ARROMANCHES

THE ARTIFICIAL HARBOURS AND ALLIED LOGISTICS

Christophe PRIME

ARROMANCHES

THE ARTIFICIAL HARBOURS
AND ALLIED LOGISTICS

OREP
EDITIONS

CONTENTS

Rolls of wire mesh were placed on the sand on Utah, to facilitate the movement of men and vehicles when they disembarked from their LSTs and LCIs. © NARA

INTRODUCTION

Nineteen forty-four was the year of all dangers, but also a year of great hopes for the Allies. To vanquish the ugly face of Nazi Germany, they would need to set foot on the old Continent and, to do so, to engage considerable technical and human resources.

It took two long years to perfect the plans for Operation Neptune, the aim of which was to enable two armies to land in Normandy and to establish sustainable bridgeheads there. The operation

implied colossal logistics, all the more so since the effort would need to be sustained and gradually increased over the months that followed, in order to support and reinforce these armies in their progression towards the frontiers of the Reich. Normandy remained the Allies' leading logistics base up to November 1944.

The aim of the present book is to offer an insight into what went on behind the scenes during the Battle of Normandy, the technical prowess in the

Dodge WC 54 ambulance belonging to the 546th Medical
Ambulance Company, landed on Omaha on the 12th of June.

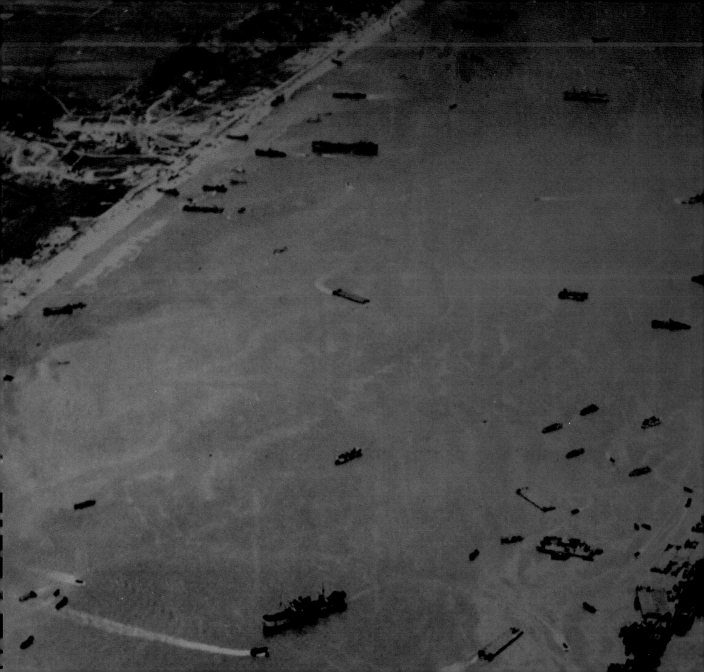

CHAPTER 1

OPERATION NEPTUNE

The first US troops landed at Lough Foyle (Ireland) on the 24th of January 1942. © NARA

A LONG AND PAINSTAKING ENTERPRISE

On the 2nd of February 1943, after six months of deadly combat, *Generalfeldmarschall* Friedrich Paulus, commander of the German 6th Army, encircled within Stalingrad, surrendered to the Soviet Army. For the first time since the start of the conflict, the *Landser* (German infantryman) discovered the bitter taste of defeat. The *Wehrmacht* permanently lost its hold in the East, after a new reverse of fortune in Kursk in July 1943. Concurrently, Joseph Stalin, at the helm in the Kremlin, increasingly firmly insisted that his Allies open a second front in the West to relieve his armies and to face the brunt of the war against Germany since the launch of operation *Barbarossa*.

However, between Washington and London, no agreement could be reached. As soon as the United States entered the conflict, the US high command began to elaborate invasion plans. The Chief of Staff, General George C. Marshall, headed for London on the 8th of April 1942 to present the British with two projects for landing operations

on the north-western European coast, aimed at nailing down the German divisions and relieving the Red Army. Operation *Sledgehammer*, scheduled for September 1942, consisted in landing on the Cotentin peninsula and recapturing the port of Cherbourg. The second operation, codenamed *Roundup*, was a larger scale enterprise involving no less than 48 divisions, 7,000 ships and 6,000 planes. It was scheduled for the spring of 1943.

Although perfectly aware of the decisive nature of any direct attack on Germany, the British Prime Minister Winston Churchill and his staff believed any such action to be, as yet, premature. The costly memories of the failed landing in Gallipoli in the Dardanelles in 1915 (46,000 dead) and their military weakness at this point in the conflict made them very doubtful as to the chances of success of such an operation.

The American war machine had been mobilised late in the conflict and was incapable of engaging in an enterprise of this scale before late 1942. President

Franklin D. Roosevelt's ambitious *Victory Program*, aimed at ensuring US supremacy in terms of weapons and ships was still in its very early days. He needed to enlist, train and equip hundreds of thousands of soldiers before sending them to fight on foreign fronts. The British were reluctant, for they knew they would have to bear the brunt of the task.

BUY WAR BONDS

This coloured poster by Newell C. Wyeth, produced in 1942, was designed to urge the Americans to help fund the war effort.

General Marshall and Henry Stimson, Secretary of War, in 1942. © NARA

Churchill, Roosevelt and their military staff meeting in Washington late 1941 to elaborate a global strategy. With Germany as the principal enemy, the battle in the Atlantic increased in intensity and the North-African landing operation was launched. © Library of Congress

August 1943, McKenzie King, Roosevelt and Churchill gathered at the Château Frontenac in Quebec. They agreed to land their armies in Europe and decided to entrust command of the operations to General Eisenhower. © NARA

A LONG DECISION-MAKING PROCESS

Following the *Acadia* conference held in Washington from the 22nd of December 1941 to the 14th of January 1942, both British and Americans agreed to open a second front in Europe. Their initial aim was to weaken Germany by means of aerial bombardment campaigns and a naval blockade. Peripheral attacks, in the Mediterranean in particular, were to force the enemy to disperse its troops. Pragmatism on the British side, along with the urgency of the military situation in the Pacific led Roosevelt to postpone operation Roundup in favour of a landing operation in French North Africa. Placed under the command of General Dwight D. Eisenhower, operation Torch proved successful (8th November 1942). Concurrently the 8th British Army defeated the *Afrikakorps* at El Alamein.

In January 1943, Roosevelt and Churchill met in Casablanca to set the basis of a joint strategy and to plan the liberation of Western Europe. They scheduled the invasion for the following year. Seven months later, the Allied chiefs gathered once more in Quebec and set the date for the combined operation on the north-west coast of France for the 1st of May 1944. In the meantime, they decided to continue their efforts in Italy. After driving the Axis forces out of Tunisia, the Allies took control of Sicily late August 1943, before setting foot on the Italian peninsula. The Salerno landings began on the 8th of September; however, fierce resistance from the Germans considerably slowed down the Allied progression.

A German tank destroyed during the offensive launched by the VIII British Army at El Alamein.

The 1st USID set foot on the shores of Oran on the 8th of November 1942.

Appointed *Chief of Staff to Supreme Allied Commander* (COSSAC) in March 1943, General Frederick E. Morgan was entrusted with preparing Overlord, a large-scale operation that would enable the Allies to set foot on the shores of Western Europe. Although the precise landing zone had not yet been determined, the invasion plan was ready by July.

During the Teheran conference (28th November - 1st December), Churchill, Roosevelt and Stalin approved the proposals put forward by the COSSAC. Eisenhower, appointed Supreme Allied Commander, arrived in England on the 14th of January 1944. He established the *Supreme Headquarter Allied Expeditionary Force* (SHAEF), whose mission was to plan and to supervise the Normandy Landings.

LE COURRIER DE L'AIR

APPORTE PAR LA R.A.F.   *LONDRES, LE 28 JANVIER 1943*

A Casablanca les Nations Unies déclarent: "Reddition sans condition de l'Axe"

LES Alliés ont tenu leur plus importante conférence de la guerre : réunis à Casablanca M. Winston Churchill et le Président Roosevelt accompagnés de leurs chefs d'Etat-Majors généraux ont, pendant dix jours, examiné la situation militaire sur tous les fronts de la guerre mondiale, et pris un parfait accord des décisions importantes ayant trait aux "campagnes offensives de l'année 1943."

SIMULTANÉMENT, LE GÉNÉRAL GIRAUD ET LE GÉNÉRAL DE GAULLE, ÉGALEMENT RÉUNIS POUR LA PREMIÈRE FOIS EN TERRE MAROCAINE, ONT CONSTATÉ LEUR ACCORD SUR L'UNION NÉCESSAIRE DE TOUS LES FRANÇAIS DÉSIREUX DE LUTTER POUR LA LIBÉRATION DE LA FRANCE ET LA DÉFAITE DE L'ENNEMI COMMUN.

A l'issue de la conférence, un communiqué a été publié, dont nous citons, les points saillants :

Pendant la conférence de presse les deux grands hommes d'état s'entretiennent confidentiellement.

Voir en page 4 d'autres photographies de Casablanca

"Le Président des Etats-Unis et le Premier Ministre de Grande-Bretagne étaient accompagnés par les chefs des Etats-Majors combinés des deux pays: pour les Etats-Unis, le général Marshall, chef d'Etat-Major de l'Armée américaine, l'amiral King, commandant en chef de la Marine américaine, le général Arnold, Commandant en Chef l'aviation de l'Armée américaine; pour la Grande-Bretagne, l'amiral de la Flotte Sir Dudley Pound, premier Lord de la Mer, le général Sir Alan Brooke, chef d'Etat-Major général impérial, le maréchal de l'Air Sir Charles Portal, chef d'Etat-Major de l'Air.

"Le vice-amiral Lord Louis Mountbatten, chef des Opérations Combinées, était également présent.

"Le Président était accompagné de M. Harry Hopkins, et fut rejoint par M. Averell Harriman, représentant spécial du Président pour les questions de Prêt-Location.

"Avec M. Churchill se trouvait Lord Leathers, ministre britannique des Transports de Guerre.

"Pendant 10 jours, les Etats-Majors combinés ont tenu constamment séance, se réunissant deux ou trois fois par jour, et rendant compte par intervalles

Pour que la paix revienne

Le Président Roosevelt a dit à la presse: "Nous avons décidé que la paix ne pourra revenir dans le monde que par l'élimination totale de la puissance allemande et japonaise. Ceci veut dire: la reddition sans condition de l'Allemagne, de l'Italie et du Japon."

Le Président des Etats-Unis a précisé qu'il n'entendait point par là la destruction des peuples des pays de l'Axe mais la destruction de leur philosophie de haine, de terreur et de domination.

La stratégie russe triomphe

LA réoccupation de Salsk, au sud-ouest de Rostoff, et d'Armavir, au nord-est de Maïkop, donne une indication précise sur la ligne directrice de l'offensive russe.

En effet, ces deux villes sont des jonctions ferroviaires importantes. Au lieu de tout risquer dans une attaque directe contre Rostoff, les Russes sont en train de couper la retraite des divers groupes d'armées opérant dans le Caucase et de désorganiser leur repli vers l'ouest.

Il semble que l'objectif immédiat des divisions russes qui se sont emparées de ces deux villes soit Tikhoretsk, dont l'occupation mettrait en péril les armées allemandes qui avaient avancé si imprudemment dans le pays du Kouban.

Ainsi, des forces ennemies importantes verraient leur retraite coupée.

Au nord de Rostoff, dans la région du Donetz, les Russes qui occupent Kamenska s'avancent vers Voroshilovgrad et Likhaya. L'occupation de ces villes menacerait sérieusement les forces allemandes du coude du Donetz. Il y a lieu de souligner toutefois que la résistance allemande est beaucoup plus acharnée dans cette région industrielle et minière. Les Allemands rendent parfaitement compte qu'en réoccupant les villes et mines du Donetz, les armées russes doubleraient leur potentiel matériel.

Ce qu'il y a d'étonnant, c'est que l'effort russe ne se limite pas à ce front sud, d'une importance vitale pour l'issue de cette campagne, ainsi que pour

SUITE À LA PAGE 2   *SUITE À LA PAGE 2*

Airborne handout dated 28th January 1943 announcing the Inter-Allied Conference held in Casablanca.

A Bren Carrier belonging to the 1st Canadian Infantry Division landing in the region of Pachino on the 10th of July 1943.

TWO YEARS' PREPARATION

The British and American forces prepared for the fray, whilst continuing ongoing operations in view of opening a second front.

After defeating Göring's *Luftwaffe* and, in doing so, warding off the threat of any German invasion, the United Kingdom set to redeploying all industrial efforts towards the mass production of military material. Over 2 million jobs were created, bringing the total number of British citizens mobilised in the army, civil defence and arms factories to 22 million. Women played a highly active role in the war effort. In June 1944, the British army had reached its maximum workforce, i.e. 5.12 million recruits, including some 450,000 female auxiliaries. With support from the Commonwealth, the nation was engaged on land and on sea (North Africa, South-East Asia). Precious material support also came from the United States in the form of the Lend-Lease Act. In Canada, industrial development reached its peak and, until such times as the United States entered the war in the wake of the Japanese attack on Pearl Harbor, the country became Britain's leading supplier of military equipment.

President Roosevelt mobilised the American people and its economy as from January 1942. The Victory Program generated millions of jobs and productivity rapidly increased thanks to systematic standardisation. In just a few months, the country became the 'Arsenal of Democracy'. Industries reconverted, automobile manufacturers interrupted civilian vehicle production in favour of armoured vehicles, trucks or artillery pieces and naval construction yards mass produced war ships of varying tonnage, tankers and cargo ships. Half of Allied weaponry was to be produced by the United States. Tens of thousands of planes and military vehicles were stored along the main road networks and near ports. A vast share of this material was designed to equip the armies of other Allied nations, including the Red Army. The US armed forces, which barely comprised 567,000 men and women in 1940, were to increase at a sustained pace. By 1944, some 13 million US citizens donned the military uniform.

The home front, highlighted in all countries, as on these British and Canadian posters.
© Library and Archives Canada

The Liberty Ships were mass produced in the Bethlehem-Fairfield naval construction yard (Baltimore).
© NARA

THE LIBERTY SHIP

In 1941, the United States launched a programme to produce a series of Liberty Ships, designated 'EC2-S-C1', and of T2 fuel tankers to compensate for the losses inflicted by the packs of German *U-Boote* and to transport ever-increasing quantities of equipment across the ocean. Henry Kaiser, a naval construction yard owner, took part production standardisation and task specialisation to their very limits. The seven elements that comprised his cargo ships were sent to one of his eighteen construction yards to be assembled in the slipways. Rivets were replaced by welding. Labourers were housed in dormitory towns and worked both day and night on a 3-shift basis. The very first ship, the Patrick Henry was launched in September 1941. As from 1943, one cargo ship was produced every 42 days, instead of the 6 months initially forecast by naval technicians. *SS Robert E. Peary* was in turn launched on the 12th of November 1942, just 4 days and 15 hours after its keel was installed. Despite their low speed and their fragility, the 2,710 ships produced enabled the Allies to compensate for the tonnage lost due to German attacks. Convoys were intensified, enabling the American Expeditionary Forces to be transferred to Great Britain. In June 1944, 574 of these ships would be needed to forward supplies to the Allied troops engaged in Normandy. *SS Jeremiah O'Brien*, berthed in San Francisco Bay, was the last Liberty Ship to take part in the D-Day Landing operation.

Insignia awarded to the American labourers who worked on the Liberty Ships. © Author's collection

Advertising for the GMC DUKW amphibious truck. © Author's collection

BT-13 training planes during assembly in the Vultee Aircraft factory. © Franklin D. Roosevelt Library

No less than 11 firms, including American Locomotive (Alco), ceased their usual production to make M4 Sherman tanks. © NARA

Soldiers from the 87th Infantry Division waiting for inspection by General Clarkson, their unit commander, 8th May 1943. © NARA

OPERATION BOLERO

Given the time it would take for the US Army to prepare to participate in a large-scale offensive in Europe, the invasion was impossible before the month of July 1943. The threat brought by the German *U-Boote* in the Atlantic, the lack of merchant ships and the dispatching of a share of the American Expeditionary Forces towards the Mediterranean and the Pacific had hindered the transfer and establishment of US troops in the British Isles.

General Henry H. Arnold, USAAF commander, was the man behind operation Bolero. The War Department's Operations Division and the USAAF headquarters devised plans to transfer 525,000 GIS, 240,000 aviators and 235,000 logistics specialists, i.e. a total of one million soldiers and 69 air groups, by the 1st of April 1943. A British and American logistics cell was entrusted with coordinating the operation from London and Washington.

The first troop movements began in April 1942, within the framework of operation Roundup. On the 31st of July 1943, only 238,000 soldiers had been effectively transferred to the British Isles. However, thanks to Ultra, the *Kriegsmarine's radio transmissions were deciphered and new anti-* submarine tactics enabled the Allies to successfully counter the U-Boote threat in the Atlantic and to increase the rate of further convoys. Within six months, 700,000 men crossed the Atlantic Ocean. By May 1944, they were 1.52 million.

P-47 Thunderbolt fighter planes taking off from Liverpool to head for the USAAF bases on the 19th of November 1943.

An Allied convoy braving the elements in the Atlantic Ocean.

The tanker *Dixie Arrow* sinking after being hit by a torpedo off the Hatteras headland on the 26th of March 1942.

On either side of the Atlantic Ocean, as factories worked at full speed, and men relentlessly trained, the military high command perfected its battle plans. Over the months, the British Isles were transformed into a gigantic patchwork of arsenals. Vast military camps, hospitals and airfields emerged. Tens of thousands of tanks, trucks and guns were gathered in open-air storage areas, along with ammunition, food and fuel. In May 1944, around 16,000 planes of all sorts could be seen, lined up along the tarmac of the makeshift airfields. Similarly, the ports now housed some 5,000 war ships and landing craft along with 1,600 merchant ships.

Installed aboard merchant ships, this zigzag convoy clock enabled crews to regularly change direction to escape the German *U-Boote*.

TARGET · ONE PORT

Whereas setting foot on the Old Continent was sure to prove a perilous task, it was but the first step towards liberating Western Europe. The success of the invasion would largely depend on the Allied armies' capacity to rapidly provide the necessary men and material to ensure the continuance of military operations on the Continent.

The bridgeheads could only be extended if troops were provided with regular supplies. Unloading transport ship cargoes directly on the beaches via barges and amphibious trucks was one way

of partially satisfying needs over the first few days. The logistics effort, that would need to be gradually intensified in line with the growth of the expeditionary corps itself, required major infrastructures. The rapid capture of a deep-water port, capable of berthing high-tonnage ships, was vital in ensuring the survival of the future bridgeheads.

However, doing so remained as yet a hypothetical possibility for the Germans had transformed the Channel and Atlantic ports into genuine fortresses

'We knew that even after we captured Cherbourg its port facilities and the lines of communication leading out of it could not meet all our needs. To solve this apparently unsolvable problem we undertook a project so unique as to be classed by many scoffers as completely fantastic. It was a plan to construct artificial harbours on the coast of Normandy.'

General Dwight D. Eisenhower *Crusade in Europe.*

Two Landsers armed with heavy machine guns guarding the entrance to a French coastal port.
© Bundesarchiv

(*Festungen*), capable of withstanding attacks from both land and sea. There was good reason to believe that the Germans would fight bitterly and, if necessary, would not hesitate to methodically destroy port infrastructures to render them of no future use to the Allies. The failed Anglo-Canadian raid in the port of Dieppe on the 19th of August 1942 had proved to be a costly lesson.

German M42 helmet.
© Author's collection

DEFEAT IN DIEPPE

In Great Britain in the spring of 1942, Rear Admiral Louis Mountbatten, Commander of Combined Operations, set the plans for an amphibious landing operation in the port of Dieppe. Encircled by high limestone cliffs, the site was highly unsuitable for any such operation; however, this secondary port in the vicinity of the English coast benefited from lesser defence compared to many other ports along the French coast. An early attempt, launched in April and codenamed Rutter, failed due to unpredictable weather conditions and the unexpected presence of the *Luftwaffe and U-Boote patrols in the sector.* After several weeks of uncertainty, the project was resumed under the codename Jubilee.

On the 18th of August, 237 ships set sail, with 963 Canadians, 1,075 Brits and 50 US Rangers on board. At 3.30am the following morning, the landing barges were put to the water. The artillery batteries and the radar station overlooking the beaches and the port were neutralised by commandos after fierce combat. The frontal attack on Dieppe was launched a little later. The German defences, as yet intact, blindly mowed down the 2,000 men from the Essex and Royal Hamilton Regiments, along with the Fusiliers Mont-Royal. Very few of them reached the wall on the foreshore. Stuck on the pebbled beach due to damage to their tracks, the Churchill tanks were incapable of covering the few infantry groups that had managed to advance as far as the town's streets. At 9am, faced with the operation's total failure, orders were given to retreat. The death toll was horrific: half of engaged troops were lost (1,050 dead, over 2,000 prisoners) and any equipment still fit for use had been abandoned on the beach.

The beach at Dieppe, strewn with bodies and wrecked tanks, 19th August 1942. © Bundesarchiv

Weymouth, April 1944. A workman stencilling painted inscriptions on the beams that were to keep the Loebnitz platforms afloat. © IWM (A 25804)

CHAPTER 2

CODENAME MULBERRY

THE IDEA OF A PREFABRICATED HARBOUR TOOK ROOT

The British Army and Navy had learned many a lesson from the disastrous outcome for the Franco-British expeditionary corps on the Gallipoli peninsula, at the entrance to the Dardanelles strait, in 1915. They had fully grasped the importance of the weather, sea conditions, knowledge of the terrain, the resources engaged and the quality and regularity of further supplies to ensure the success of a combined operation.

In July 1917, Winston Churchill, who was Minister of Munitions at the time, had put forward the idea to invade the German islands of Borkum and Sylt from the sea, in order to form an artificial harbour by sinking flat-bottomed concrete barges. Later evolution in the conflict had rendered the project obsolete. To this very day, no document relating to this project has ever been found.

In December 1940, Guy Maunsell, the engineer who had designed the impressive Maunsell Forts – armed towers protecting the Thames estuary – was contacted by Lieutenant-Colonel Wilson from the War Office. He asked Maunsell to study the feasibility of an artificial harbour. In return, Maunsell drafted a report entitled Emergency Port Works, in which he proposed the use of concrete caissons to create a harbour capable of safely welcoming transport ships, but his project was rejected.

Early 1941, the Transportation 5 (Tn5) department was created within the War Office and placed under the orders of General Major D.J. McMullen. The department was in charge of military engineering and port maintenance. Bruce White, the chief engineer, was entrusted with the mission of building military ports in Great Britain and of working on the concept of an artificial harbour. As the months went by, Churchill became increasingly impatient. On the 30th of May 1942, he drafted a note in which he stressed the absolute necessity to bring the project to fruition.

PIERS FOR USE ON THE BEACHES

C.C.O. or Deputy
They must float up and down with the tide.
The anchor problem must be mastered.
Let me have the solution worked out.
The difficulties will argue for themselves.
Winston Churchill
30.5.42

A few days after Dieppe, Vice-Admiral John Hughes-Hallett, commander of the naval forces during the raid, declared that, if a port could not be captured by the Allies, it would need to be taken across the English Channel.

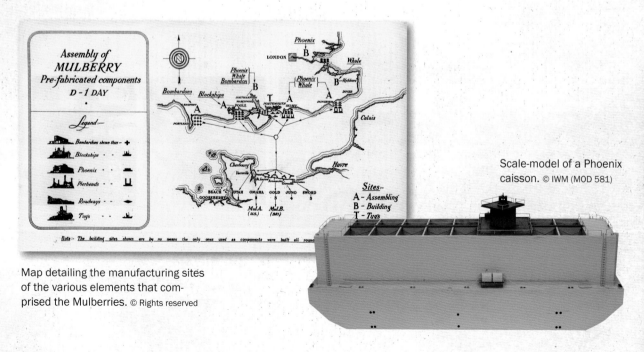

Map detailing the manufacturing sites of the various elements that comprised the Mulberries.

Scale-model of a Phoenix caisson. © IWM (MOD 581)

Lieutenant General Frederick E. Morgan, chief of the COSSAC, donning the SHAEF insignia on his shoulder.

Lord Louis Mountbatten, captain at the time, in the company of other officers on the deck of the destroyer *HMS Kelvin*. © IWM (A 661)

'If we can't capture a port we must take one with us.'

Lord Louis Mountbatten.

During a briefing, the Welsh engineer Hugh Iorys Hughes put forward the idea of building a port from separate elements that would be transported in the vicinity of the future invasion zone. His idea consisted in creating a port that was protected from the sea swell by artificial breakwaters. Within the resulting harbour, unloading platforms linked by a one kilometre-long jetty would enable cargo and troop transport vessels to moor. Floating causeways were to provide a link between these platforms to dry land. This revolutionary concept involved a port that, rather than being set on the sea bed, would float and would move in time with the tide and the swell.

Built in a series of separate elements, this huge meccano set was to be towed across the English Channel then assembled in the future landing zone. This seemingly ludicrous idea nevertheless aroused Churchill's curiosity for he asked Lord Louis Mountbatten, commander of Combined Operations, to study the feasibility of such a plan. He presided over the Rattle conference held in Largs in Scotland from the 28th of June to the 2nd of July 1943. Around fifty American, British and Canadian officers gathered at the *Hollywood Hotel*. The Allied planners chose Normandy as the landing zone and began to study the creation of artificial ports, whilst deploying operation Fortitude, a military deception aimed at leading the German high command to believe that the landings would take place elsewhere.

Promoted to the rank of Naval Chief of Staff for planning operations around Operation Overlord, Hughes-Hallett attended the Quadrant Conference in Quebec in August 1943, to have the plans for the future artificial harbour ratified by the participating heads of state. Admiral Mountbatten gathered his own team in the bathroom. The paper ships that floated in the bath tub were quick to sink under the effect of the lapping water. He then used a lifebelt to create a protective harbour.

Given the lack of transport barges among the Allied naval forces, the construction of artificial harbours was deemed essential for mooring high tonnage ships. An estimated 38,000 to 40,000 tonnes would need to be transported to the bridgeheads every day in order to keep the armies sufficiently supplied.

Royal Navy officer's cap.

GIANT MECCANO SETS

Three prototypes were designed. In Conwy Morfa, in North Wales, the engineer Hugh Iorys Hughes developed a Hippo platform and a system of floating Crocodile causeways. Ronald Hamilton, an employee within the department in charge of developing secret weapons, designed a Swiss Roll floating causeway in hardened canvas tautened by cables. Lieutenant-Colonel William T. Everall and Major Allan Beckett in turn proposed a Whale floating pier. Another engineer, Pearson Lobnitz, designed a concrete Pier Head platform measuring 70 metres by 20. Weighing in at 1,100 tonnes, it slid along four 30 metre steel beams that were placed on the sea bed. It moved up and down in time with the tide. Hydraulic jacks enabled a clearance of 5 metres.

The same year, prototypes were transported to Scotland to be subjected to a series of tests, in the utmost secrecy. Wigtown Bay, located between Garlieston and the Isle of Whithorn bore many similarities with the future landing sector in Lower Normandy. The port elements were assembled nearby in Cairn Head and Rigg Bay. Extensive security measures were implemented. The local population was totally unaware of these rather strange goings on.

The two Crocodile floating causeways failed to convince, whereas the three Hippo unloading platforms obstinately refused to follow the movement of the tide. The Swiss Roll floating causeways were unable to withstand the weight of a seven tonne vehicle. On the 23rd of June 1943, all these prototypes suffered storm damage. They were all abandoned in favour of Beckett's Whale which had remained intact. In the wake of the same storm, the British engineers decided to design huge cruciform floating barriers, referred to as 'Bombardons' and aimed at protecting the future artificial harbours.

The War Office's Transportation 5 department was entrusted with the mission of building these ports, referred to as Mulberries. The Royal Navy was in turn in charge of transporting the various port elements. Their construction was supervised by the

210,000 tonnes of steel and 1,000,000 tonnes of concrete.

Combined Operations Headquarters.

Despite the terrible shortage of skilled workers in the United Kingdom since the start of the war, 45,000 labourers were successfully mobilised to bring this gigantic project to fruition. Most of them were totally oblivious to the actual purpose of their work. Over the weeks, 213 alveolated concrete caissons were built in the naval construction yards along the Rivers Clyde and Thames, the largest elements being prepared in the ports of Weymouth and Southampton. The caissons came in six different sizes. Their weight varied from 1,672 to 6,047 tonnes.

The talented Scottish artist Muirhead Bone (1876-1953), member of the War Artists Advisory Committee and a Ministry of Information employee, offered this sketch of labourers busy working on the Phoenix caissons on the banks of the Thames.
© IWM (ART LD 4333)

A total of 50 Bombardon breakwaters, 23 Pier Head platforms, 16 kilometres of Whale floating causeways, 8 unloading ramps and 670 Beetle floaters (200 made of steel and 470 of concrete) were built by thousands of labourers in Morfa, Richborough, Southsea (Portsmouth) and Marchwood (Southampton).

A total of around 300 companies, such as Balfour *Beatty, Costain, Nuttall, Henry Boot, Sir Robert McAlpine and Peter Lind & Company contributed towards the vast enterprise.* Day after day, the huge meccano sets took shape. And it was all happening according to schedule.

The SHAEF planned to install two artificial harbours that were to feed the Allied war machine over several months. Mulberry A was to be set up before Vierville/Saint-Laurent-sur-Mer, whereas Mulberry B was headed for Arromanches-les-Bains. These locations had been chosen based on the nature and the depth of the waters around them, which had been painstakingly studied by teams of frogmen for over two years.

The *Luftwaffe* reconnaissance planes had, of course, spotted these strange constructions; however, failing any further information, the German high command was incapable of fathoming out their nature and their purpose.

BUILDING THE MULBERRIES

April 1944 – Beetles and Loebnitz platforms under construction near Southampton. © IWM (A 25807 and A 25808)

Phoenix caissons under construction at the Surrey docks in Rotherhithe to the south-east of London. © IWM (H 37607)

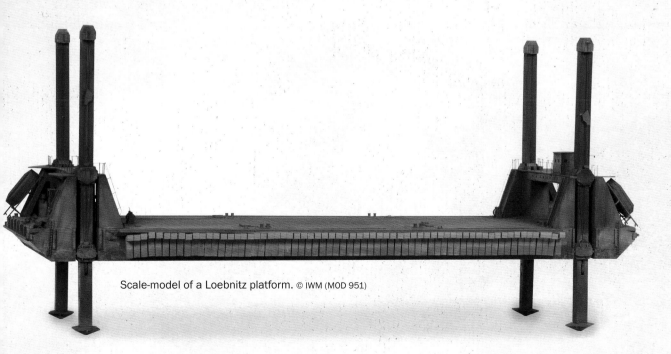

Scale-model of a Loebnitz platform. © IWM (MOD 951)

Over two months, a successive flow of scientists headed for the modest cabin in Short Lake House to test the effects of the tides and the waves on the elements that would comprise the artificial harbour.

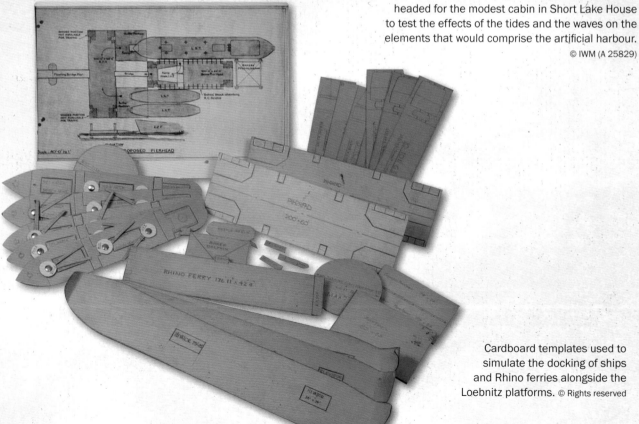

Cardboard templates used to simulate the docking of ships and Rhino ferries alongside the Loebnitz platforms.

Lieutenant R.A. Lochner from the Royal Navy Volunteer Reserve (RNVR) hard at work at Short Lake House, near Weymouth. © IWM (A 25826)

Three WNRSs repainting the ML195 launch at the *HMS Tormentor* base. © IWM (A 19496)

SECRET MISSIONS

The Allies needed to gather great quantities of information before choosing the best sites to install the artificial harbours and to ensure the feasibility of future operations. Deficient knowledge of the sea bed, in particular the presence of natural obstacles (shallows, sandbanks), but also of currents and of the beach itself (sand composition, slope), could lead to disaster. As from 1940, small British teams led reconnaissance raids along the French coast aimed at selecting the most propitious sectors for future amphibious operations. A team of hydrographers was recruited within the framework of operation Neptune. The 712th Survey Flotilla, operating from the naval base *HMS Tormentor* on the River Hamble, was trained to draw up accurate maps of the sea bed along the Normandy coast.

Operation KJF, on the night of the 26th to the 27th of November 1943, was its first mission. Three modified Landing Craft Personnel (Large) were towed 20 miles off the Calvados rocks. The craft were equipped with silencers that died down the sound of the engine. They were also equipped with sonar, probe reels and a GEE radio navigation system. The zone that was to house Mulberry B, in Arromanches and Saint-Côme-de-Fresne, was sounded. Samples were taken from the sea bed and the currents were analysed.

On the night of the 1st to the 2nd of December, the same team headed 12 miles further west to the future location of Mulberry A (operation KJG). Unfortunately, radio hitches and confusion between the Vierville church spire and the tower on the Pointe de la Percée headland led Lieutenant Berncastle somewhat astray. Sounding was conducted 2 kilometres further east than planned. By the time he realised, it was too late to correct the error, for dawn was fast approaching. Due to poor weather, certain craft took 24 hours to return to Newhaven.

Two further hydrographic reconnaissance missions were organised on the night of the 25th to 26th (Bell-Push Able) and the 28th to 29th of December (Bell-Push Baker).

Arm insignia worn by the British commando troops.
© Author's collection

This Landing Craft Personnel Large 141 is identical to those used by the 712th Survey Flotilla. © IWM (A 24658 LCP L)

LCPL141

POSTAGE ABLE

On New Year's Day 1944, the *Combined Operations Assault Pilotage Parties (COPP)* team n°1, *comprised of Major* Logan Scott-Bowden from the Royal Engineers and Sergeant Bruce Ogden-Smith, landed near Ver-sur-Mer to take measurements and samples of sand. The two men returned to Newhaven safe and sound with their precious load.

Then, within the framework of operation Postage Able, the Royal Navy developed the X-Craft, a midget submarine. On the 16th of January, *HMS Dolphin* secretly left Gosport. It was towing *HMS X-20*, commanded by Lieutenant Ken Hudspeth from the Royal Australian Naval Volunteer Reserve (RANVR). The submersible operated for two days off Luc-sur-Mer before heading to the west of Port-en-Bessin. By day, it lay on the sand a few hundred metres from the shoreline and its crew kept watch over the German defences using a periscope. By night, Scott-Bowden and Ogden-Smith donned their wetsuits and left the sub. They

A surfaced midget submarine. © IWM (A 21701)

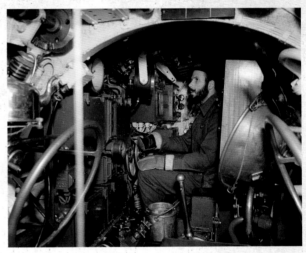

Space was extremely limited aboard the Royal Navy's X-Craft midget submarines. © IWM (A 26933)

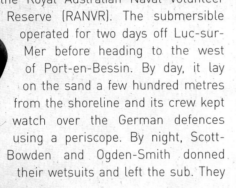

Major Logan Scott Bowden on a mission in the Gold Beach sector within the framework of operation Bell-Push Able. © COPP Heroes

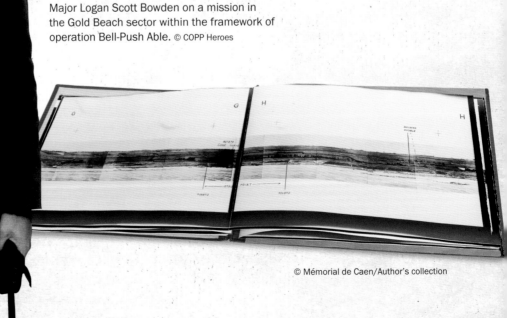

© Mémorial de Caen/Author's collection

silently swam to the shore, then meandered their way through the obstacles and sentries taking measurements and samples of sand and gravel. On the 21st of January, the exhausted crew was repatriated to England. One final operation (Bell-push Charlie) was launched on the night of the 30th to 31st of January; however a medley of fog and over-vigilant enemy sentries obliged the British forces to abandon the mission.

Thanks to the results yielded from these missions, 2 scale models of the beaches were produced. The first was installed in room 474 at the Metropol Hotel, a room occupied by the War Department, whilst the second was taken to Winston Churchill's office in the Cabinet War Rooms. A large-scale reproduction was built at Cairnryan to enable specialists to test the efficiency of landing techniques.

THE COPP

Although the early missions were conducted empirically with very basic equipment, two years later Lord Louis Mountbatten created the Combined Operations Assault Pilotage Parties (COPP). This small special force was placed under the orders of Lieutenant Nigel Clogstoun-Willmott. Ten teams of two commandos were formed. Each team was comprised of a combat swimmer and a soldier or officer from the Royal Engineers. They generally began their crossing aboard submarines, to continue towards the coast in canoes. They took geological samples and collected information on the German defences. The COPP organised several missions to Sicily and India throughout the year 1943, before taking part in preparations for Operation Neptune.

Special kapok wetsuit worn by COPP divers. Its many pockets contained the necessary tools for them to accomplish their missions, in particular an automatic pistol, a dagger, a compass and a flask of brandy. A white board attached to the wrist and a soft lead pencil enabled the COPP divers to write underwater. © IWM (UNI 3914)

In the control room in Dungeness, a panel on the wall was used to monitor the quantity of fuel currently in transit inside the pipelines under the Channel.

ANOTHER PROJECT: PLUTO

Bringing fuel into the operation zone was of vital importance to the Allies. They needed to invent ingenious systems to continuously provide for their armies.

In April 1942, Lord Mountbatten began to contemplate on the possibility of installing an underwater pipeline across the English Channel. Despite the difficulty of such an enterprise, Geoffrey Lloyd who was in charge of the Petroleum Warfare Department, nevertheless ensured him of its feasibility. Clifford Hartley, chief engineer for the Anglo-Iranian Oil Company, was appointed at the head of the project. His plan was to design a pipe that was flexible yet solid enough to withstand the currents. It would need to be capable of transporting huge quantities of fuel under extremely high pressure over one hundred kilometres. To achieve a flow of 500m³/day, i.e. 25,000 jerrycans, over a distance of 64 kilometres, a 3 inch pipe and a pressure of 100 bars were required.

Clifford Hartley put together a team of specialists from the petroleum industry, in submarine cable manufacturing and a number of military Engineers to deploy this system on the battlefield. On the 15th of April 1642, after some trial and error, in partnership with Siemens Brothers, Hartley proposed to build semi-rigid hollow tubes that were similar to the underwater cables already used for telephone transmission. They were comprised of lead and steel casings. To withstand the pressure, the tube was to be filled with water and each section was insulated by means of rupture discs.

A prototype was built in the strictest secrecy; baptised HAIS (Hartley Anglo-Iranian Siemens), it was capable of transporting 135m³/day over a distance of 32 kilometres. Its diameter was two inches (7.5cm). On the 10th of May, one kilometre of pipeline, connected to high-pressure pumps, was successfully tested on the River Medway. Then, in December 1942, six 48-kilometre pipes

These seemingly innocent seafront houses dating from the 1920s, housed pumping stations. These installations were later camouflaged.

were installed across the sea, from Swansea to Ilfracombe. Although relatively flexible, the drawback of the HAIS was its heavy weight (34 tonnes/km). The raw material it would have required forced the British to look for an alternative solution.

A second system, named HAMEL, was consequently developed. The name came from those of its designers, H.A. Hammick, chief engineer for the Iraq Petroleum Company, and B.J. Ellis, chief oil field engineer for the Burmah Oil Company. The two men decided to use 3 inch pipes in low-carbon steel. The 12 metre sections needed to be welded to obtain the necessary length. The HAMEL system was more rigid and only weighted 10.9 tonnes per kilometre.

In May 1942, the prototype was tested, first in the River Medway, then – the following month - in deeper waters in the Firth of Clyde. This life-size test highlighted the necessity to maintain a constant pressure of 7 bars to ensure the pipe's resistance. Production was officially launched on the 14th of August. The HAMEL system was finally

chosen. However, the engineers decided to use HAIS sections at the end of the pipeline. Stewarts & Lloyds (Corby) was the company entrusted with manufacturing the HAMEL pipelines, whereas Siemens Brothers (Woolwich) looked after the terminals. Over 200 kilometres of HAIS and HAMEL oil pipelines were produced on either side of the Atlantic.

In 1943, Donald Banks took the reins of the Pluto (Pipelines Under the Ocean) project and launched Operation Bambi. Production began in April. Over and above installation equipment, specific barges containing connection and pumping equipment were also built A whole network of oil pipelines was installed in Great Britain in order to supply the departure points of these underwater pipes. A pumping station, designed to drive the fuel inside the pipelines, was installed in the ruins of the Royal Hotel in Shanklin; 28 other pumps, camouflaged so they would look like simple seafront buildings, were built in the utmost secrecy in Shanklin and Sandown.

This segment of HAIS pipeline offers an insight into the different layers of material required to offer the necessary flexibility and robustness to withstand the pressure of the sea water.

'We need to use a flexible, strong and heavy tube, to avoid the effect of the current. We just need to take an underwater telephone cable from which we have removed the copper core and kept the protective lead and steel casings. Then we will have obtained a heavy tube that will remain stable on the sea bed.'

Clifford Hartley, April 1942.

The front turrets, housing 356 mm guns,
aboard *USS Nevada* (BB 36), firing against the
German defences that protected Utah Beach.
© USN/NARA

CHAPTER 3

THE BATTLE OF THE BRIDGEHEADS

THE PLAN

For the landings, the Allied command defined five perfectly distinct sectors along the Lower Normandy coast. To the east, Utah Beach and Omaha Beach were assigned to General Omar N. Bradley's 1st US Army, whilst, to the west, Gold Beach, Juno Beach and Sword Beach were assigned to General Miles Dempsey's 2nd British Army.

Located on the east coast of the Cotentin peninsula, the Utah sectors stretched across 5 kilometres of dune, from Saint-Martin-de-Varreville to Sainte-Marie-du-Mont. The COSSAC's initial plans included no landings on this eastern Cotentin coast. It was only in 1943 that the SHAEF decided to add an extra beach to the west of the Bay of Veys, in order to rapidly recapture Cherbourg. The VII US Corps, commanded by General-Major Joseph L. Collins, was entrusted with the mission of establishing contact with the airborne troops dropped further inland and the troops landing on Omaha Beach, in order to isolate the Cotentin peninsula, then to head for the port of Cherbourg.

Omaha Beach stretched across the Bessin coast over a distance of 7 kilometres from the Pointe de la Percée – to the west – to a hamlet named La Révolution, to the east. General-Major

American officers studying in detail the maze of hedges and paths directly inland from Omaha. © Magnum

Leonard T. Gerow's V US Corps was entrusted with the double task of attacking Omaha Beach then of advancing to the Isigny-Trévières-Vaucelles line, located a dozen kilometres inland.

In contrast with the American sectors, which were not continuous, the beaches in the Gold, Juno and Sword sectors stretched along a vast 40 kilometres from Port-en-Bessin, to the west, to Ouistreham, at the mouth of the Orne to the east.

Insignia of the 21st Army Group, commanded by General Bernard Law Montgomery. © Author's collection

Insignia of the Supreme Headquarters Allied Expeditionary Force. Created in December 1943, it was in the form of a Norman shield. The black background symbolised the Nazi oppression; the flamed sword of freedom surmounted with a rainbow with the colours of the Allied nations represented hope and the turquoise arch, peace that was to be restored. © Author's collection

The beaches assigned to British units were on either side of Juno Beach, the Canadian sector. To the west, Gold Beach stretched from Port-en-Bessin to Ver-sur-Mer and was assigned to General G.C. Bucknall's XXX British Corps. Its mission consisted in capturing Arromanches and Port-en-Bessin, then in crossing the River Seulles to take up position on the RN13 main road before, finally, entering Bayeux. The I Corps (British) was to land on Juno and Sword Beach before recapturing Caen as early as the evening of the 6th of June.

In May 1944, the decision was made to precede the amphibious landing operation by an airborne attack. The 6th British Airborne Division was entrusted with covering the east flank and capturing the bridges over the Orne and the canal from Caen to the sea, by neutralising the German artillery battery in Merville. To the west, the paras from the 82nd US Airborne Division were to jump in the region of Sainte-Mère-Église. The division was to gain control of this market town, along with the two bridges over the River Merderet, in order to block any German counter-attack and to free the road towards Cherbourg. The men from the 101st US Airborne Division were in turn given the mission to secure the upper causeways leading to Utah Beach, whilst neutralising enemy strongpoints. Later, they were to recapture the town of Carentan.

The full staff of the SHAEF. From left to right: General Bradley, Admiral Ramsay, Air Chief Marshal Tedder, General Eisenhower, General Montgomery, Air Chief Marshal Leigh Mallory and General Bedell Smith. © NARA

Two bulldozers trying to clear a path between the foxholes, as the columns headed inland via corridors cleared of mines. © NARA

32,000 men, 3,200 vehicles and 2,500 tonnes of equipment landed on the 6th of June.

UTAH

The landings on Utah beach were to begin at 6.30am, i.e. an hour before the British troops, due to delayed tides and the specificities of the sea bed. Over the night, the 101st and 82nd Airborne Divisions (AB) were parachuted around Sainte-Mère-Église to pave the way for future units.

The German artillery batteries and coastal defences were bombarded by Task Force 125 and the 9th USAAF's B-26 Maurauder bombers. At 6.30am, with support from Sherman Duplex Drive (DD) tanks, General Raymond O. Barton's 4th Infantry Division (Ivy Division) set foot on the Sainte-Marie-du-Mont beach, in front of the La Madeleine dunes. When the ramps of the 20 LCVP that transported the first wave of assault were lowered, the dreaded deluge of enemy gunfire simply didn't happen. Due to strong coastal currents, the barges had drifted 2 kilometres to the south of the planned landing zone and had ended up in a less defended sector. Stunned by the bombardments, the German defenders in *WN 5*, the main defensive position in the sector, were quick to surrender.

The beach and exists were cleared in barely an hour and, at 11am, in Poupeville, the junction was successfully made with advanced units from the 101st Airborne. The missions entrusted to the 4th USID met with equal success and with very few losses. A total of 197 men were wounded, dead or unaccounted for. Northward progression was slowed down by the Saint-Marcouf and Azzeville batteries. However, the junction with the 82nd AB remained to be made in the Sainte-Mère sector. The VII US Corps prepared for its next missions: to recapture the town of Carentan and the port of Cherbourg.

Naval Amphibious Forces insignia.
© Author's collection

A shell, fallen a few dozen metres from these Ivy Division infantrymen, sitting against the anti-tank wall. © NARA

Two seamen and a medic from the 2nd Naval Beach Battalion at rest alongside the *WN 5* communication bunker. © NARA

Exit E-1, right next to *WN 65* established in the Ruquet sector. The bunker, housing a 50 mm gun, was reused as a communication post by the Engineers. © NARA

OMAHA

Omaha Beach forms a 7 to 8 kilometre indentation flanked on either side by cliffs and before which stands a 60 metre escarpment. Four valleys offer access to the small towns of Vierville, Colleville and Saint-Laurent. In 1944, this extremely well-defended sector was far from propitious to an amphibious attack.

As for Utah, the landings were scheduled at 6.30am. Aerial and naval bombings had landed off target, leaving the German defences virtually intact. Furthermore, the *352. Infanterie Division*, a powerful unit, had been despatched to the sector. The 1st and 29th US Infantry Divisions, commanded by Generals Clarence Charles Huebner and Gerhardt, together with Lieutenant-Colonel James Rudder's Rangers Force, had been chosen to take control of the beach.

When the barges became within 400 metres of the shore, deadly enemy fire showered down on the assault infantry and engineer troops. The amphibious tanks that had not sunk became the target of anti-tank guns. From one end to the other of the beach, German guns, mortars and machine guns whipped the sand with fearsome accuracy. The following waves of assault sustained almost equally heavy losses. Vehicles and men became packed on the incessantly narrowing line of sand, as the tide gradually rose. Total chaos reigned on Omaha, until a few infantry groups finally reached the heights. Attacked from the rear, the German strongpoints then fell, one after another. A little further west, the Rangers had successfully taken control of the artillery position established on Pointe du Hoc and had neutralised the 155mm guns that had been concealed in a nearby orchard.

34,000 men and 3,400 vehicles landed on the 6th of June.

Omaha Beach on the 7th of June. Unloading the barges proved a difficult task at high tide. Cases of supplies and buoys accumulated here and there. The bodies of lost soldiers were attached to stretchers. © NARA

On the evening of D-Day, the German army had lost the battle on Omaha Beach; however, the situation remained extremely precarious for the V US Corps. The inland advance had barely gained 2 kilometres. The enemy dug in its heals. The human toll was of 4,720 killed, wounded or unaccounted for.

Five infantry regiments were out of action, but the artillery, the DCA (anti-aircraft defence) and the logistics units had not yet engaged in the operations. Barely 100 tonnes of supplies of the required 2,400 had been landed.

Heavy helmet bearing the insignia of the 5th and 6th ESB, operating on Omaha, presented alongside demolition equipment. © Mémorial de Caen/Author's collection

GOLD

Gold Beach lies fifteen kilometres to the east of Omaha. Only its lower sandy and gently sloping sector was propitious to an amphibious assault. The cliffy western side was totally impassable.

With support from the 8th Armoured Brigade, General-Major Douglas A.H. Graham's 50th Northumbrian Infantry Division set foot on French soil before Asnelles and Ver-sur-Mer at around 7.25am. They landed around an hour after their American counterparts due to differing tides. The German defences put up fierce resistance at the

Men from the n° 47 Commando disembarking from their LCA near La Rivière.

extremities of the landing sector. However, the fortified positions in La Rivière and Le Hamel were finally neutralised thanks to special tanks. The troops thrust forward and advanced 20 kilometres inland. The 47th Royal Marine Commando (RMC) advanced over a distance of 13 km towards Port-en-Bessin. The 69th Infantry Brigade in turn secured the east flank and, at dusk, joined forces with the Canadian troops who had landed on Juno Beach. At dawn the following day, the men from the 56th Infantry Brigade entered Bayeux without resistance, whilst the 2nd Devonshire took control of the Longues-sur-Mer artillery battery. The vast majority of predetermined objectives had been achieved.

MkII helmet belonging to the Hampshire Regiment. Its owner, a rifleman by the name of J. Dowell, was taken prisoner in Normandy and sent to a *Stalag* in Poland.

Assault vest made by M&Co in 1943.

25,000 men, 2,100 vehicles and 1,000 tonnes of equipment landed on the 6th of June.

THE LIBERATION OF ARROMANCHES

The 231st Brigade landed at Asnelles (Jig Beach sector) at around 7.30am. The two regiments met with perilous conditions on either side of the La Roquettes sector. A 1st Battalion Hampshire Regiment company neutralised *WN 36*, however subsequent progression was stopped by *WN 37*. Losses rapidly increased. Several officers were out of action. Tanks belonging to the Sherwood Rangers sank, became stuck in the sand or were destroyed by German guns. The Dorsetshire Regiment's 1st Battalion managed to break through the German defences and to wriggle its way out of the marshland minefields. The *WN 37* resistance nest was reduced to silence by a bull's eye shot from a Sexton self-propelled gun The British troops finally liberated the village of Asnelles after an hour's combat before continuing their advance towards Arromanches. The 1st Hampshire Regiment in turn silenced *WN 38* in Saint-Côme-de-Fresné, followed by the *Kriegsmarine radar station located on the plateau*. The British troops could finally enter Arromanches late afternoon.

A 7th British Armoured Division, 22nd Armoured Brigade armoured column leaving Gold Beach on the 7th of June. © IWM (B 5251)

JUNO

The Juno sector stretches across a distance of 7 kilometres between Saint-Aubin and Courseulles-sur-Mer. The orders received by General-Major Rodney F.L. Keller's 3rd Canadian Infantry Division were to progress towards Caen as far as Authie, then to take control of the Carpiquet airfield. This 10 kilometre-long beach was far from propitious for a landing operation. The presence of high rocks on the sea bed between Graye and Saint-Aubin-sur-Mer meant that the Allies would need to wait for the tide to be high enough to safely pass them.

Scheduled at 7.45am, the assault was led by the 3rd Canadian Infantry Division's 7th and 8th Infantry Brigades. Support was provided by the 2nd Canadian Armoured Brigade and the 48th Royal Marines Commando.

The barges that transported the first wave of assault landed 20 minutes behind schedule. The partly submerged obstacles caused minor losses. The Canadian troops landed on either side of the River Seulles. The Canadian infantry was given a hard time. Although the arrival of tanks enabled the Canadians to exit the beach, it took several hours of fierce combat before they could drive out the German defenders entrenched in the nearby

Insignia worn by the men from n°7 Beach Group, landed on Juno. © Author's collection

villages. With the rising tide, the beach had become increasingly cramped, men and vehicles finding themselves in heavy jams.

Combat gradually moved inland over the hours to follow. The Canadians had advanced as far as Caen and Carpiquet. The villages of Creully, Colomby-sur-Seulles, Anguerny, Colomby-sur-Thaon, Fontaine-Henry, Villons-les-Buissons and Anisy were liberated; however, neither Authie nor the airfield had been reached, nor had the junction been made with the Northumbrian Infantry Division,

© Library and Archives Canada

21,500 men, 3,200 vehicles and 2,500 tonnes of equipment landed on the 6th of June.

Beach Groups gathering together prisoners and tending to the wounded at Bernières-sur-Mer. © Library and Archives Canada

landed on Gold. To the east, the 48th Royal Marines Commando was stopped in its tracks at Langrune-sur-Mer. A 4 kilometre-wide corridor still separated the Juno and Sword bridgeheads. Located around the village of Luc-sur-Mer, this gap was a genuine threat, for it offered a propitious terrain for an enemy counter-attack. And indeed, elements from the *21. Panzer Division* reached Luc-sur-Mer in the afternoon, before turning back. The 3rd *Canadian Infantry Division had lost 961 men and the British 270.*

Sten MkII submachine gun and Canadian military bandage produced in Toronto in 1944.
© Author's collection

SWORD

The most easterly assault sector stretched across a distance of 8 kilometres from the village of Saint-Aubin-sur-Mer to the mouth of the Orne. However, the presence of high rocks on the sea bed prevented any landing barges from accessing the Oboe, Peter and Roger sectors at the western extremity of the Queen sector. The sector immediately to the west of the mouth of the Orne canal, between Langrune and Ouistreham was solidly fortified.

Sword Beach was assigned to General-Major Thomas G. Rennie's 3rd British Infantry Division. Armoured support came from the 13th and 18th Royal Hussars. The 41st Royal Marines Commando (RMC) and Lord Lovat's 1st Special Service Brigade also took part in the assault.

They landed before Hermanville-sur-Mer and Colleville at 7.25am, after naval and aerial bombing. The rapidly rising tide prevented demolition teams from clearing the obstacles on the beach, whilst unloaded vehicles accumulated on the foreshore as they waited for exits to be cleared. Bitter fighting ensued opposite the locality of Hermanville-la-Brèche and Ouistreham, where the 1st Special Service Brigade distinguished itself. The French *Fusiliers Marins* from n°4 Commando neutralised the bunker at the casino.

Late afternoon, the advanced British units came face to face with a counter-attack by the *21. Panzer Division*. Some German armoured units reached the shoreline before turning back. At the centre of the operation, a vast share of troops from the 3rd British Infantry Division – hindered by the German strongpoints they encountered along their way – were within a few kilometres of Caen, but had not been able to take control of the town as initially planned. The 9th Infantry Brigade was in position on the Périers-sur-le-Dan ridge, and the 185th was in turn in control of the bridges over the Orne. Lord Lovat's commandos, along with the 45th RMC, had successfully joined forces with the 6th Airborne paras at the Bénouville bridge. Conversely, the 41st Royal Marines Commando was at a standstill before Lion-sur-Mer and Luc-sur-Mer. It was only to successfully join the 48th Royal Marines Commando, landed on Juno, the following day. A total of 630 men from the Iron Division were killed, wounded or unaccounted for.

28,845 men and 2,603 vehicles landed on the 6th of June.

Churchill Petard tank belonging to the 5th Assault Regiment and Bren Carriers, stuck in their tracks on Sword Beach pending any possible inland advance. Amidst the sand, the men sought shelter from the German shells that continued to shower across the beach. © IWM (B 5085)

Men from the Royal Engineers (n°6 Beach Company), 84th Field Company with their assault equipment, advancing towards the Queen sector. The nurses are taking care of wounded and sick soldiers.

Assault gas mask issued to the Anglo-Canadian troops

Ammunition case for a 25-pounder Howitzer.

Sections of floating piers were towed
across the English Channel. The men on
board kept watch to ensure operations
went smoothly. © IWM (B 5689)

Loebnitz platforms approaching the Normandy coast. © IWM (H 39297)

OPERATION CORNCOBS

On the 30th of May 1944, a week prior to the D-Day Landings, 55 old warships and cargoes (22 British, 16 American and 14 of other nationalities) were taken to Loch Linnhe in Scotland. Their crews were sworn to secrecy as the ships prepared for their ultimate mission. They were mined and ballasted with concrete. All identification was removed and only a number was indicated on the lateral side of the bridge. Escorted by ten tugboats and six corvettes, the ships set off on the 31st of May on their way to Poole Bay where three further ships joined them. They then began their Channel crossing, before being scuttled in the deep waters before the five landing beaches. The operation was commanded by the Royal Navy Lieutenant-Colonel Landsdowne.

On the 4th of June 1944, as the Allied armada gathered in zone Z (codenamed Picadilly Circus) off the Isle of Wight, orders were given to prepare to transport the 400 elements that comprised the Mulberries. Some 158 tugboats were required to accomplish this mission. A total of 15 kilometres of Whale piers and 33 Loebnitz platforms were towed across the Channel. Around 40% of the floating causeways were lost during the crossing.

The 146 caissons that had been submerged pending D-Day were brought afloat and gathered together in Lee-on-Solent. The US Navy Captain Edward Ellsberg, a specialist in refloating ships, was in charge of supervising the operation. The daunting concrete structures were towed across the Channel, over a distance of 160 kilometres, by 85 tugboats. Given the weight and the fragility of these elements, the crossing was made at an average speed of 4 knots (8 km/h).

Kapok life jacket found after the D-Day Landings.
© Author's collection

GOOSEBERRIES

The first blockships were scuttled as from the 7th of June, one kilometre from the beaches. Because of the tides, Operation Corncobs needed to be completed by D+2; however, technical hitches, German artillery fire and nocturnal incursions by the *Luftwaffe obliged the Allies to postpone positioning any further ships*. The last vessels were finally scuppered on the 10th of June. The Bombardons were moored offshore.

Civilian crews were transferred to tugboats, leaving only military crews on board to serve the anti-aircraft defence guns. The explosives that had been loaded into the ships' double bottoms were electrically detonated from the bridges. The flow of water was accelerated by opening the normally watertight doors and by means of holes made in the partitions. Their holds filled with concrete, the ships gently sank and hollowed their bed in the sand. The grounding depth was designed to leave the hulls 2 metres above the water level at high tide.

The lines of scuttled ships formed artificial sea walls referred to as Gooseberries. They were designed to enable small craft and mid-tonnage

US Navy US M1 helmet, easily recognisable thanks to its grey-blue stripe. © P. Gage collection

cargoes to unload men and material on the beach, sheltered from the sea swell, as early as D+2. The soldiers and seamen working within the harbour took up quarters in the cabins on the upper decks of the ships used as control centres, maintenance bases, repair zones, rest areas and care centres. Before the shores of Hermanville-sur-Mer, the French battleship *Courbet* continued to fly its

The Rhino ferry RHF-19 unloading GMC and Dodge trucks on Omaha Beach on the 10th of June 1944. The Royal Navy's *LCT-502* can be seen doing likewise in the background. © USN/NARA

Rhino ferry crews operating in the Omaha sector lived aboard the blockships that were still equipped with light anti-aircraft guns. © USN/NARA

flag and was still equipped with its anti-aircraft weapons.

Over the first days following the landings, the Gooseberries at Omaha and Utah were to respectively handle 3,000 and 2,500 tonnes. The metal causeways were used to unload coasters and small barges, whereas the DUKWs and the Rhino ferries provided shuttle services between the beaches and the ships offshore.

Despite harassment from the German artillery, on the 16th of June (D+10), 5,736 tonnes were effectively landed on Utah and 9,008 on Omaha. The Gooseberries on Gold and Juno also handled ever-increasing quantities. The same day, some 7,717 tonnes of equipment were unloaded there.

Cranes unloading barges in Courseulles harbour.
© IWM (A 24241)

THE ROLE OF THE LOWER NORMANDY PORTS

Use was also made of the small fishing ports along the Normandy coast. Coasters and low-tonnage cargo ships unloaded 8% of total daily traffic in these ports. Grandcamp-Maisy harbour was operational as from the 17th of June, handling an average of 280 tonnes per day, whereas 475 tonnes were unloaded in nearby Isigny. At the end of the month, the two ports had dealt with some 3,500 tonnes of freight per day. Saint-Vaast-la-Hougue, Barfleur and Carentan were also put to use by the Americans. Concurrently, from the 12th of June to the 25th of September, 111,500 and 94,000 tonnes were respectively unloaded in Courseulles and Port-en-Bessin by the British. By mid August, these small Norman ports collectively handled an average of 8,800 tonnes of material every day.

A fleet of active barges around the blockships 577 (George W. Childs) and 578 (*Artemus Ward*) that protected Gooseberry G-2 off Omaha. © IWM (A 24167)

BLOCKSHIPS

G-1 Utah Beach, Sainte Marie-du-Mont

Blockships: SS Benjamin Contee, SS David O. Saylor, SS George S. Wasson, SS Matt W. Ransom, M.S. West Cheswald, M.S. West Honaker, SS West Nohno, SS Willis A. Slater, SS Victory Sword, SS Vitruvius, SS Sahale.

G-2 Omaha Beach, Saint Laurent-sur-Mer

Blockships: SS Alcoa Leader, SS Artemas Ward, H.M.S. Audacious, SS Baialoide, HMS Centurion Courageous, SS Exford Flight-Command, SS Galveston, SS George W. Childs, SS Kentuckian, SS Kofresi, SS James W. Marshall, SS James Iredell, SS Illinoian, SS Lena Lickenbach, SS Maycrest, SS Olambala, SS Potter, SS Robin Gray, SS Stanwell, SS West, SS Grama, SS Wilscox, SS West Nilus.

G-3 Gold Beach, Arromanches/ Asnelles-sur-Mer

Blockships: SS Alynbank, SS Alghios Spyrido, SS Elswick Park, SS Flowergate, SS Giorgios P., SS Ingman, SS Innerton, SS Lynghaug, SS Modlin, SS Njegos, SS Parklaan, SS Parkhaven, SS Winha, SS Bosworth, SS Parklaan, SS Saltersgate, SS Empire Bittern, SS Sirehei, SS Vinlak, SS Winha.

G-4 Juno Beach, Courseulles-sur-Mer

Blockships: SS Belgique, SS Bendoran, SS Empire Bunting, SS Empire Flamingo, SS Empire Moorhen, SS Empire Waterhen, SS Manchester Spinner, SS Mariposa, SS Panos, SS Vera Radcliffe, HMS Dragon, SS Norjerv.

G-5 Sword Beach, Hermanville-sur-Mer

Blockships: SS Becheville, Courbet, SS Dover Hill, HMS Durban, SS Empire Defiance, SS Empire Tamar, SS Empire Tana, SS Forbin, HNLMS Sumatra.

US Navy ribbed overall and lamp.
© Mémorial de Caen/Author's collection

Telephone cables being installed aboard a blockship. © IWM (A 24076)

Blockship 571 (SS *Alynbank*) immediately after being scuttled before Gooseberry G-3 on Gold Beach.

CONCRETE SHIPS OFF THE NORMANDY COAST

Although Henry Kayser and the Liberty Ships went down in legend by contributing towards the success of the Allied victory in the Atlantic and the Pacific, the concrete ships fell into oblivion. In 1917, several countries began to build ferroconcrete ships. The United States rekindled the project in 1942 in order to increase the tonnage of its merchant fleet by replacing steel with concrete. Their reinforced concrete hulls proved to be both resistant and lightweight. The floating Phoenix caissons were built following the same principle.

The first ships left the yards in Tampa Bay as from 1943 at a pace of one per month. These ships weighed in at 4,690 tonnes for a length of 110 metres and a width of 16 metres. The 24 vessels produced were named after illustrious personalities from the cement industry. Very few know that SS David O. Saylor and SS *Vitruvius* ended their short careers as blockships. Shortly after being brought into service late 1943, the two ships were sent to Liverpool. They were scuttled off Utah beach on the 16th of July 1944.

THE BRIDGEHEAD JUNCTION

On the evening of the 6th of June, the Anglo-Americans had failed to achieve all their targets. Only the troops landed on Gold and Juno had successfully joined their bridgeheads. On the 7th of June, the 50th British Infantry Division entered Bayeux, which had remained intact, to continue their inland progression whilst constantly endeavouring to make contact with the Americans who had landed on Omaha. On their way, 5 kilometres to the west of Arromanches, they effortlessly sealed the surrender of the garrison in position at the Longues-sur-Mer coastal artillery battery.

The Americans landed on Omaha launched reconnaissance operations towards Port-en-Bessin in an aim to reach the British troops, whilst continuing their attempts to enter into contact with their compatriots landed on Utah. The junction was finally made a few hours after the capture of Port-en-Bessin by the Royal Marines n°47 Commando. Hence, on the 8th of June, the Allies were in control of a 60 km line of coast stretching from the Orne to the Vire estuary. Together with Courseulles,

An M7 Priest self-propelled gun from the 2nd US Armoured Division on its way through Carentan. © NARA

captured almost intact by the Canadians, the Anglo-Canadian divisions now had control of two ports. Churchill landed in Courseulles on the 12th of June and, two days later, General de Gaulle in turn set foot on French soil.

Also on the 12th of June, the V US Corps, landed on Omaha, crossed the River Vire and made contact with Collins' troops, landed on Utah. Thanks to this junction, the bridgehead had reached a length of 80 kilometres and a depth of 20 on the most advanced front towards Caumont - Saint-Lô. The American paratroops took control of Carentan the same day.

1st US Army and 2nd British Army insignia.
© Author's collection

It took two days to land an infantry division. Here, the last units from the 50th British Infantry Division set foot on Gold Beach. © IWM (B 5133)

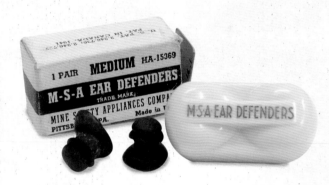

Ear plugs for artillery gunners.
© Mémorial de Caen/Author's collection

A Royal Winnipeg Rifles (7th Brigade, 3rd Canadian Infantry Division) column advancing inland.
© Library and Archives Canada

INSTALLING THE MULBERRIES

The first 61 metre-long and 18 metre-high Phoenix caissons came within view of the Normandy coast on the morning of the 6th of June 1944. They were positioned by tugs before being immersed, by opening the floodgates, at high tide on the morning of the 7th. The highest parts formed an efficient protective barrier. Some of them were surmounted with platforms housing Bofors 40mm guns to ensure the harbour's anti-aircraft defence.

Platforms weighing 1,100 tonnes and measuring 70 metres by 20 metres were placed inside the harbours. They were used as unloading docks or as pierheads. Designed by the engineer Pearson Loebnitz, these platforms moved in time with the tide by sliding along four large 30 metre-high metal beams which were placed on the sea bed. This ingenious system avoided having to interrupt unloading operations.

The link between the docks and dry land was ensured by 28-tonne interconnecting metal causeways placed on 19-tonne steel or concrete floaters.

Two men opening the valves that would flood and sink this Phoenix caisson. In the background, the alveolated structure, ladders and rulers enable the structure's immersion to be measured. © IWM (A 24358)

A floating causeway under construction off Arromanches.
© IWM (A 24162)

SHAEF planners had 8 days of supplies stored on ships and barges. The artificial harbours were designed to handle 7,000 tonnes of freight per day. After a 13-day transition period, the Liberty Ships began to bring in supplies for the bridgeheads. In theory, the harbours were to ensure the vast share of supply provision for combat units as from D+41.

The artificial harbours needed to be operational at D+21, i.e. the 27th of June.

On Omaha, the 25th US Naval Construction Regiment had doubled its efforts. Mulberry A was making great progress. The Bombardons, the 15 blockships that comprised Gooseberry G-2, 34 Phoenix caissons, one floating causeway and two Loebnitz platforms were installed. LST 342 was the first to berth on the 16th of June.

Lieutenant-Colonel Mais' n°1 Port Construction and Repair Group was entrusted with building Mulberry B, in Arromanches. By the 10th of June, 15 blockships and 20 Phoenix caissons were in place. The central dock, which at this stage

British Royal Engineers flag flying above Mulberry B over the summer of 1944. © IWM (FLA 5499)

only comprised two platforms and one floating causeway, was completed mid July. The east and west docks were complete or on the verge of completion. The semi-immersed Swiss Roll was only installed in September. The harbour, which was baptised 'Port Winston', was fully operational as from the 23rd of June. In the meantime, the barges and DUKWs successively headed for Arromanches beach.

Sappers destroying part of the coastal sea wall to the west of Arromanches, where a floating causeway is due to be installed. © IWM (A 24158)

THE STORM OF THE CENTURY

By the 18th of June, 314,000 men, 40,500 vehicles and 116,000 tonnes of material had been landed on Utah and Omaha. Concurrently, the British and Canadian units had landed 211,000 men, 28,600 vehicles and 100,000 tonnes of supplies. However, Allied logistics were far from at full pace and traffic remained 25% under target. It was to drastically fall due to the storm.

In the English Channel, the weather took a brutal change for the worse on the morning of the 19th of June. Force 6 and 7 north-easterly gales swept across the Normandy coast. Ships and barges were tossed in all directions in the 2 to 3 metre troughs. A convoy of floating piers sank in the Channel along with its tugboats. Unloading operations were reduced by 60% and the naval troops forced to leave their ships to take refuge on dry land. The elements unleashed their wrath for 72 hours. Around 800 ships and barges of all tonnages were grounded, including 320 LCTs.

US Navy seamen trying to secure a barge in the midst of the storm. © USN/NARA

When the storm reached its peak, the ships and barges were thrown against each other off Omaha Beach.
© USN/NARA

Construction of Mulberry A, in Saint-Laurent, had made less progress than the British harbour and suffered more serious damage. The Bombardons were torn from the anchor points and were sent drifting onto the caissons, opening huge gaps where waves several metres high came thrusting forth. Of the 31 Phoenix caissons installed, 27 were seriously damaged or destroyed. Several blockships had also moved.

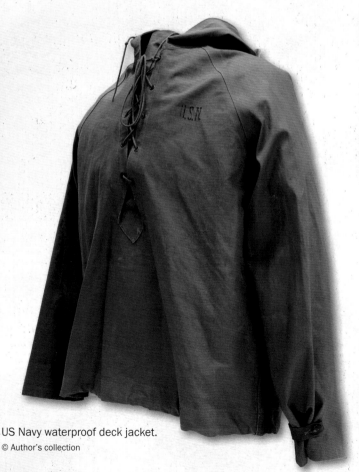

US Navy waterproof deck jacket.
© Author's collection

After the lines of Bombardons were dislocated, the caissons and the blockships bore the full brunt of the huge crashing waves. Large-tonnage ships outside the harbour dragged their anchors.

Within these harbour 'walls', the floating causeways had been damaged by the swell and by drifting vessels. The precious Rhino ferries and the 286 vessels of all sorts were driven onto the shore. The harbour elements, pontoons and craft formed an inextricable entanglement of metal carcasses. Utah suffered lesser damage. The breakwaters and causeways were in a poor state and 212 barges had grounded.

Benefiting from better shelter, Mulberry B in Arromanches, together with the Anglo-Canadian Gooseberries, had been subjected to less destruction. The British had taken great care when assembling their Mulberry, contrary to their US Navy counterparts who had preferred speed over caution.

On the 21st of June, the worst day of the storm, 4,250 tonnes of material were unloaded in Normandy. Throughout the three days of stormy weather, from the 19th to the 22nd of June, the American and British units respectively unloaded 12,255 and 17,265 tonnes.

BOMBARDONS THAT PROVED INEFFECTIVE

These 61 metre-long and 7.6 metre-wide cruciform hollow metal caissons were positioned offshore of the artificial harbours and the beaches. Their role was to break the sea swell. Their lower cavities were filled with 2,000 tonnes of water, whereas the upper cavity contained watertight cases. The Bombardons were attached to each other by means of chains. These daunting structures were designed to reduce wave amplitude by 40%; however, their effectiveness had been jeopardised. Indeed, they had been placed on the wrong spot and in one single line, as opposed to the planned two lines.

On the 21st of June, the F-class destroyer *HMS Fury*, an El Kebir, Dakar and Arctic Convoys veteran, damaged by an underwater mine, ended its career at the foot of the Arromanches cliffs.

A SERIOUS HINDRANCE

The 1st US Army and the 2nd British Army took supplies from the stocks that had been patiently gathered over the two previous weeks – stocks that seemed to melt like snow. Although food supplies sufficed, the Allied command was obliged to ration its divisions' consumption in ammunition, the artillery in particular. Plans were modified accordingly. Bradley decided to postpone the VIII CAUS offensive to the south of the peninsula, in order to enable the VII CAUS to take control of Cherbourg. Dakota planes belonging to the 9th Tactical Air Command were chartered to transport ammunition. Hence, every day, 500 tonnes were brought in by air.

> **Admiral Ramsay, Commander-in-Chief of the Allied Naval Expeditionary Force, estimated that 83,000 men, 20,000 vehicles and 140,000 tonnes of supplies had failed to be brought to the bridgeheads due to the storm.**

All efforts were made for traffic to be resumed as quickly as possible. On the American side, Engineer battalions cleared the heaps of twisted metal and the entangled pontoons, and cut up the wrecks. The Seabees repaired the damaged Rhino ferries, whilst the Coast Guards repaired the barges. The most severely hit vessels were towed back to England. Clearing work took a whole week. The US Navy organised for Landing Ship Tanks (LSTs) to unload directly on the beaches. These striking 100 metre-long ships were grounded on the sand. Once empty, they were to wait for high tide before heading back out to sea.

US Navy barge rudder wheel.
© Omaha Beach Memorial Museum

Crafts of all sorts, reduced to wrecks along the pebbled shores of Omaha. © NARA

The great violence of the waves dislocated the floating causeways on Mulberry A. Reinforced and anchored, those on Mulberry B put up better resistance. © NARA

Construction of the harbour resumed after the storm.
The LST quayside was completed on the 17th of June.
© IWM (BU 987)

Several methods were employed to accelerate loading the trucks.

Mulberry A was abandoned and efforts thereafter concentrated on Mulberry B. Recoverable elements from the former - around 30% of the total - were used to repair the latter. A dozen new blockships and 26 Phoenix caissons were towed across the Channel to fill the gaps in the Gooseberry from the 7th of July to the 26th of August 1944. Two floating causeways were also installed opposite Le Ruquet and Colleville. Rhino ferries and DUKW trucks provided a continuous shuttle service between the beach and the transport ships, whilst the largest LSTs continued to ground at low tide to unload. Although more rudimentary, these methods yielded remarkable results, as did the use of secondary ports. Port infrastructures were active on a round the clock basis, an infernal pace both for men and machines, but providing supplies and reinforcements could not be neglected.

These efforts were to prove fruitful, for the week after the storm, the tonnage unloaded on the American beaches was above the SHAEF's most optimistic forecasts. An average of 11,000 men, 2,000 vehicles and 8,000 tonnes of material and supplies had been brought to shore each day on Omaha. Results for the Utah Gooseberry were slightly inferior with a daily average of 7,500 men,

800 vehicles and 5,500 tonnes of material. It took a few weeks before the backlog was fully recovered, the relatively stagnant front enabling armies to reduce consumption.

US Army wooden chest with a bar code comprised of three coloured stripes. The code was designed to facilitate identification of the equipment belonging to a given company and transported by sea.

THE SPECIALISTS

Over a period of five months, the beaches and the harbour in Arromanches became the very lung of the Allied armies. Activity was so intense that the Normandy shoreline now resembled a huge bee hive.

Material and men transhipment operations required flawless organisation and skilled personnel. Each army had its own special units in charge of accomplishing the many missions relating to port activities on the beaches and in the artificial harbours.

G-1 Utah: *1st ESB*

G-2 Omaha: *5th and 6th ESB*

G-3 Gold (King, Jig sector): *n° 9, n° 10 Beach Groups*

G-4 Juno (Mike, Nan sector): *n° 7, n° 8 Beach Groups*

G-5 Sword (Queen sector): *n° 5, n° 6 Beach Groups*

The American and British armies respectively entrusted these missions to the Engineer Special Brigade (ESB) and the Beach Groups. They landed in the early hours of the 6th of June, at the same time as the assault troops.

The men were to remove the obstacles and mines strewn across the beaches and exits, to supervise landing operations for men, vehicles and supplies, to create fuel, food and ammunition depots along with assembly points for freshly landed units. Their duties included traffic control by land and by sea, together with signposting, evacuating the wounded and prisoners of war. They were also to defend the beaches against any enemy incursions and to prevent other risks, including fire for example. These units included a multitude of specialists.

They were assisted by naval troops who were in charge of coordinating maritime operations and links with the ships moored offshore. On the American side, the Naval Beach Battalions and the Seabees played an essential role. They cleared and marked out navigation channels, unloaded vessels and evacuated the wounded.

Men from the 1st ESB, recognisable via the blue semi-circle painted on the helmets, posing willingly for the photographer. This brigade, reuniting 7,400 men, was attached to 90 Engineer units, Supply Corps units, port and transport companies. © NARA

The Royal Engineers and the Beach Groups busy clearing Sword Beach. © IWM (B 5116)

On the British side, the Royal Navy provided each brigade with a 3,000-man Beach Group. Over and above an infantry battalion for close protection, the Beach Group reunited units specialising in transmissions, medical care, pioneering, mechanical and electrical engineering, anti-aircraft defence, transport and port management. The Royal Engineers corps was also fully involved in these operations.

THE SEABEES

Created in January 1942 by Admiral Ben Moreell, the US Navy naval construction force was engaged in the Pacific isles and during amphibious operations in European theatres. The corps, which comprised sixty different professions, was in charge of repairing or building port infrastructures, bridges and airstrips. Their official motto was *Construimus, Batuimus (We build, We fight)*.

MkII helmet belonging to a Beach Group, easily recognisable thanks to its white stripe.
© Author's collection

Engineer Special Brigade insignia. © Author's collection

THE THREAT OF THE *KRIEGSMARINE*

Despite great efforts, the Germans failed to thwart the Allied war machine. The *Kriegsmarine thrust its meagre forces into the battle; however, the Allied navies and aviation were on the lookout.* The losses sustained were far from shaking the Allied supremacy.

The U-Boote (submarines) and *S-Boote* (E-Boat – *fast attack craft) were serious threats the Allies had to guard against.* On the 6th of June, there were no German ships at sea due to a storm that had lasted several days. Three *Torpedosbooten* (torpedo boats) brought in from Le Havre, retaliated in the morning, sinking the Norwegian destroyer *Svenner.* Hounded by the Coastal Command patrol planes and the Royal Navy fighter groups, the *U-Boote* from the *Landwirt Gruppe* were unable to enter the Bay of Seine, where the Allied armada was positioned. Only the ships equipped with *Schnorchel* continued to operate in the English Channel. Over the following nights, *Kriegsmarine* surface vessels conducted raids and sank a few barges and LSTs on their way across the Channel. On the 9th of June, 2 LSTs were sent to the sea bed off La Hague. The frigate HMS *Blackwood* was damaged the following day by *U-764*. On the 15th, *U-621* sank a 1,490-tonne LST. Three frigates were sunk in the immediate wake. Only 5 of the original 36 *U-Boote* were still operational.

The recapture of Cherbourg and bombardments on the ports of Le Havre and Boulogne, on the 14th and 15th of June, reduced the threat posed by the *Kriegsmarine*. The ships that had escaped these events were forced to seek refuge in Belgian ports.

The *Schnellboote* fleets positioned in Le Havre and Cherbourg were a genuine threat for the Allied ships sailing through the Bay of Seine. © Author's collection

Nocturnal operations continued throughout the month of July. Late July, 25 ships including HMS Frobisher and two destroyers, were sunk by German *S-Boote*. To limit further risks, the Germans launched large numbers of long-range torpedoes against the Allied traffic, but with little success. Minelayers intervened regularly. After the 23rd of August the *Kriegsmarine withdrew its last remaining vessels to the Netherlands and Germany.*

One last and dramatic episode took place on the night of the 24th to the 25th of December 1944, when the cruise ship *SS Leopoldville* was hit by a torpedo launched by *U-486* off Cherbourg. Of the 2,000 men from the 66th USID on board, 736 were killed and 493 were never found.

Personal effects belonging to a *Kriegsmarine* crew. © Vassas collection, Mémorial de Caen/Author's collection

Cockpit of a surfaced Neger human torpedo. © Bundesarchiv

THE *K-VERBAND*

The Germans then engaged the *K-Verband*, a unit specialised in the use of Marder midget submarines, Neger human torpedoes and Linsen radioguided explosive boats. Their *K-Fottillen* were based in Honfleur, Houlgate and Fécamp. Eight attacks engaging several dozen of these devices were launched against the Allied fleet. On the night of the 5th to the 6th of June, 24 Neger torpedoes were fired. They sank two minelayers, *HMS Magic* and *HMS Cato*, but only nine human torpedoes successfully returned to base. The following night, 21 Negers were deployed off Sword Beach. This time, they were located, and pursued. They nevertheless managed to add the minelayer *HMS Pylades* and the Polish cruiser *HMS Dragon* to their toll. Another destroyer, *HMS Isis*, was sent to the sea bed during an ultimate attack on the 16th of August. The meagre Germans successes were of no comparison to the extremely heavy losses sustained. On the night of the 2nd to the 3rd of August, 58 Marder belonging to *K-Flottille 362* and 22 Linsen explosive boats from *K-Flottille 211* were launched between Houlgate and Trouville against the ships moored off Port Winston. A violent battle ensued, causing heavy losses on both sides. LCG1 and the ML 131 launch engaged a Marder, in vain. At 3.10am, a torpedo came close to hitting the destroyer *HMS Duff*. At 3.25am, the destroyer *HMS Quorn*, the armed trawler *HMS Gairsay* and *HMS LCT 764* were all sunk by Marders. The troop transport ships Fort de Lac and Samlong were both damaged, whereas the Liberty Ship SS Samtucky was sent to the depths. Damage to the light cruiser *HMS Durban* was such that it was transformed into a blockship. At 6.10am a Marder was in turn sunk by the *HDML 1049* launch. The destroyer *HMS Blenathra* captured another Marder intact, however a handling error led to the torpedo exploding, causing serious damage. Then one more Marder was captured intact. Escapees were pursued by RAF Squadron 132 Spitfires. Only 17 out of 158 Marders returned to base.

THE *LUFTWAFFE* INCURSIONS

A 40 mm artillery piece installed aboard HMS Bulolo.
© IWM (A 24 399)

that protected both ports and ships. These silver-coloured balloons were filled with gas and held in place by means of cables. Positioned at regular intervals and varying heights, they were designed to hinder German planes. Decoys were also installed to mislead German crews, whereas artificial fog was created around Mulberry B in Arromanches at nightfall. Any intruders within the zone were welcomed by the anti-aircraft defence guns. The batteries defending the fuel port in Port-en-Bessin entered into action a total of 33 consecutive nights – proof, if need be, of the genuine threat posed by the *Luftwaffe*. Over 5,500 shots were fired and 11 German planes brought down.

The results yielded by the *Luftwaffe* were no more glorious than those of the *Kriegsmarine*. On the 6th of June, sixty fighter planes made a total of 275 flights. Very few managed to approach the beaches, under permanent protection by clouds of Allied fighters. By night, bombardiers and torpedo bombers specialised in anti-naval combat, based in the south of France, took over. The German craft were very rapidly detected on the Allied radars. They needed to fly at very high altitude to avoid the hundreds of VLA (Very Low Altitude) Balloons

The *Luftwaffe* was particularly active by night. Junkers Ju 88 and Dornier Du 217 bombers attacked the beach sectors and moored ships, with a few highly successful bull's eye hits. One of these bombs hit the Liberty Ship *SS Charles Morgan* on the 10th of June. The Germans also used Henschel 293A radio-controlled glide bombs. On the 9th of June, one of these weapons sank the destroyer *USS Meredith*.

The Germans laid a number of acoustic and magnetic mines that were extremely difficult to detect. These insidious weapons inflicted minor losses on the Allied fleet. They damaged or sank several transport ships and warships. On the 7th of June, the destroyer *USS Tide* sank with its crew and its load on the Banc du Cardonnet sand bank, after

The 34 Phoenix caissons that comprised Mulberry B were all surmounted with a Bofors 40 mm gun. © IWM (B 5726)

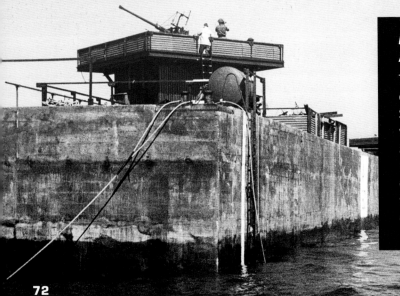

MULBERRY B AND ITS DAUNTING ANTI-AIRCRAFT DEFENCE

The 76th Anti-Aircraft Brigade was in charge of defending Gold Beach and the artificial harbour. Seven 'DCA' heavy anti-aircraft defence batteries were established on dry land. The cruiser *HMS Despatch*, 15 DCA barges, 3 blockships, the Phoenix caissons and the quayside were all equipped with anti-aircraft guns. The arsenal was quite impressive: 56 3-inch guns, 84 Bofors 40 mm gun, 36 Polsten 20mm guns.

PROVIDENTIAL TARGETS

Totally oblivious to their purpose, the German air and naval forces continued to hound the blockships. The Liberty Ships George S. Wasson and Benjamin Contee were also bombed 32 times from the 7th to the 14th of June, whereas the Liberty Ship Matt W. Ransom was bombed up to ten times. On the night of the 7th to the 8th of July, the French battleship *Courbet was the target of Neger human torpedoes operating from* Villers-sur-Mer. Even the blockships retaliated. The cargo ship *Vitruvius and the fuel tanker Victory Sword both shot down six enemy planes on the 10th of June.*

hitting an influence mine. Then on the 8th, *USS Rich* was reduced to ruins after detonating three mines of the same type, killing 91 seamen. On the morning of the 24th of June, as the *Derry Cunihy*, moored off Ouistreham, set sail, it set off the explosion of a German pressure mine. The ship was literally split in two. The 43rd Wessex reconnaissance regiment on board was annihilated (182 dead and 150 wounded). The cruiser *HMS Frobisher* was damaged on the 18th of July, then sunk by an *S-Boote on the 9th of August*. The minesweepers worked relentlessly to clear the English Channel.

Land-based depots were also choice targets for, given their density, the pilot's chances of striking a bull's eye were high. On the night of the 11th to the 12th of June, a German bomb destroyed one of these depots in Formigny. Nevertheless, despite its great efforts and sacrifices, the *Luftwaffe* was incapable of countering the increasingly powerful 21st Army Group.

A JU-88 A-2 bomber plane with its fuselage painted black preparing for an assault mission. © Bundesarchiv

JU-88 toolbox. © Vassas collection/Author's collection

THE *LUFTWAFFE* INTRUDERS

On the 2nd of August 1944, an Arado 234 twin-jet bomber used for photographic reconnaissance took off from the RN44 main road near Juvincourt. Lieutenant Erich Sommer's Ar 234 *Blitz* (lightning) slipped its way behind the Allied lines. Its 12,000 metre altitude and its speed offered protection from any anti-aircraft defence and from Allied fighter planes. Its cameras enabled it to take pictures of the harbour in Arromanches and the surrounding airfields. The plane managed to return to base without incident. A dozen similar missions were launched up to the 12th of August. Although they offered the *Luftwaffe* more information than during the first two months, it only confirmed what the German command already knew.

Fliegerbluse and flying bonnet belonging to a *Luftwaffe* pilot and non-commissioned officer. © Vassas collection/Author's collection

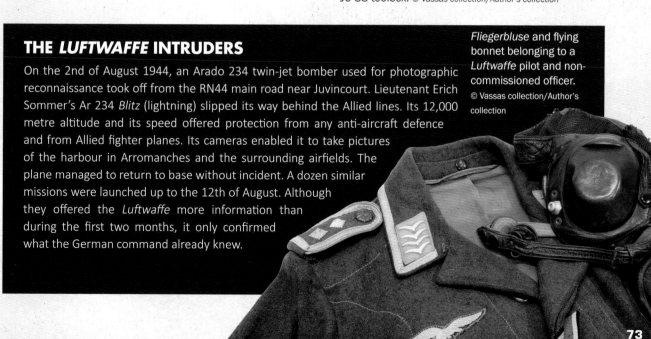

RECONQUERING CHERBOURG

After improving the situation on Omaha and sealing the junction with the American infantry and airborne troops, the VII Corps successfully isolated the Cotentin peninsula and reached Barneville on the 18th of June, encircling 40,000 Germans in the process. The stopper in Montebourg fell the next day. Bradley ordered General Collins to begin his northward advance to Cherbourg. Making rapid progression, his divisions liberated Bricquebec then Valognes, encountering virtually no opposition; however, German resistance increased on the approach to the Norman port. The VII Corps launched its attack on the 22nd of June with an aerial bombardment aimed at destroying German units. General Von Schlieben, commander of the German garrison, was in no way deluded as to the chances of withstanding the Allied assault, but he had received orders from the Führer to defend to the bitter end and to abandon to the enemy, not a port but a pile of ruins.

On the 25th of June, as the warships engaged in a duel with the German coastal batteries defending the internal harbour and the fighter-bombers pounded the land-based defences, the

The fall of the fortress of Cherbourg was a major break-through. *The Courrier de l'Air* newspaper issued on the second week of July highlighted the event. © Mémorial de Caen

General Joe Collins, Commander of the VII US Corps, at Fort du Roule. © NARA

A column of German prisoners heading for Paris under close supervision. © NARA

infantry gradually infiltrated the town. After bitter confrontation, the Americans were finally in control of the town on the 26th of June. The Fort du Roule, a strategic fortification, fell the following day and Von Schlieben was taken prisoner along with 1,600 of his men. On the 30th of June, the American troops obtained the surrender of the 6,000 Germans that were entrenched in the La Hague headland. A total of 39,000 Germans were taken prisoner. On the Allied side, there was a heavy toll of 25,000 killed or wounded.

In liberated Cherbourg, the church bells resounded joyfully for the first time in four years. The triumphant US generals were acclaimed by thousands of Cherbourg locals who had gathered in front of the town hall.

A GI from the 79th USID advancing towards Cherbourg. © NARA

DESTRUCTION OF THE PORT

The 1st US Army had managed to take control of a major continental port, even if its capture was sealed over a week after the SHAEF's provisional programme.

Although the Americans were aware that the enemy may well have rendered the port unfit for use, they were nevertheless staggered by the damage sustained. The men from the *Kriegsmarine* had implemented a systematic destruction plan. Hitler awarded Hennecke with the Knight's Cross of the Iron Cross for what he referred to as a feat unprecedented in the annals of coastal defence.

One officer from the US Engineers described it as '... a masterful job, beyond a doubt the most complete, intensive and best-planned demolition in history'. The detonation of explosive charges placed in blast holes hollowed out under the quay facings had blown them to smithereens. The railway tracks had been torn up and wrecked cranes were strewn across the ground. The reclaimed land zone was riddled with craters and cluttered with the damaged *blockhaus*. The wet docks and passes were blocked with wrecked barges, tugboats and trawlers. The wrecks of the Norwegian whaler *Solgimt* and the coasters *Grandlieu* and *Wormand* prevented any access to the commercial port and the transatlantic dock. Cranes and freight wagons lay in the depths of the port. The swing bridge that once linked the town's two districts was also unfit for use. The marine terminal and the Amiot factories had been blown up with dynamite. Magnetic, acoustic, pressure and electromagnetic pulse bombs and booby traps of all sorts had been placed in the silt or under rolls of barbed wire to prevent them being defused.

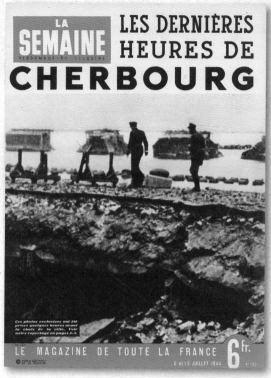

The *La Semaine* magazine, issued on the week of the 6th to the 13th of July, featured the town's recapture on its front page.
© Mémorial de Caen

Access to the commercial port was blocked by the wreck of a 960-tonne coaster.
© NARA

The Germans had methodically destroyed the port infrastructures, the arsenal and the transatlantic dock. Allied bombing had completed the job.
© NARA

77

REPAIRING THE DAMAGE

The destruction of the port was a serious problem for the American command which fully intended to repair damage so that the facility could rapidly resume service and increase its logistic capacity to allow the 1st US Army to compensate for lost time.

Bringing the port and its infrastructures back into working order was a challenge for the US Navy and US Army teams. The American forces were to demonstrate all the scope of their skills in the field.

Colonel James B. Cress's 1056th Engineer Port Construction and Repair Group was kept hard at work. It was assisted by three Engineers divisions. The engineers defined which sectors were priorities and the port's future organisation: the Napoleon beach for DUKW amphibious trucks, the wet dock in the commercial port for barges, the reclaimed land for the LSTs and the Homet sea wall for the Liberty Ships and those transporting locomotives and wagons. They were confident and estimated that, following repair work, the port's daily capacity could reach 17,900 tonnes.

Royal Navy minesweepers began to clear the outer harbour on the 2nd of July. Deep-sea divers were needed to clear the basins, the docks and the mooring points. Around 80 British, American and

British seamen equipping the deep-sea divers in charge of clearing the port. © NARA

'The hard we shall do today, the impossible we shall do tomorrow.'

The motto of the US Army Engineers.

even French divers volunteered, working in lines to probe the silt, marking mines and underwater obstacles on their way. They cut up metal using oxyacetylene torches. Teams worked relentlessly by day and by night.

Over a hundred scuppered ships were brought to the surface. The men repaired the gaps in the quayside, repaired the roads and railway infrastructures. No less than 80 Bailey bridges and 4,750 tonnes of material were required. New hoisting and stevedoring machines were brought in from the United States and installed. Wooden docks were built by Engineers teams along the reclaimed land zone and the wet docks for unloading barges and coasters. One of the Bailey bridges was used to replace the destroyed swing bridge. Numbers of civilians and German prisoners of war took part in clearing operations.

On the 13th of July 1944, a navigation channel was opened between the Fort de l'Ouest and the Napoleon beach. Three days later, four Liberty Ships moored in the outer harbour. Since no docks had yet been brought back into working order,

Royal Navy deep-sea divers' insignia. © Author's collection

their cargoes were unloaded by DUKWs directly onto the Napoleon beach, which had been cleared and organised accordingly. Although still limited, port traffic was nevertheless resumed. An average of 12,000 tonnes of goods were handled every day throughout August. It was only on the second fortnight in September that the port had finally reached its full capacity. The greatest tonnage was unloaded in November: 19,955 tonnes.

On the 31st of July, the first LST LSD-21 unloaded wagons on the Tourlaville beach under the gaze of the Afro-American soldiers from the Transportation Corps.
© NARA

Soldiers landing in Cherbourg. Their kit bags are marked with the unit's bar code. © NARA

A P-38 Lightning fighter plane from the 367th Fighter Group at the A-21 airfield in Saint-Laurent-sur-Mer. © NARA

THE CONTRIBUTION FROM THE AVIATION

For the SHAEF, the construction of airfields on the continent was an absolute necessity in order, not only to ensure that the Allied fleet and ground troops benefited from aerial protection, but also to contribute towards logistics. Given the few existing airfields in Normandy (Carpiquet, Lessay, Querqueville...), and their occupation by German troops, the SHAEF planned to create new airfields from scratch.

During the first days of the invasion, Allied planes had no choice but to shuttle between their bases in south-east England and the bridgeheads. However, the first airstrips were operational as from the 10th of June. Initially, three 600 metre-long Emergency Landing Strips (ELS) were created within the narrow bridgeheads to house damaged planes. The first official airfield was established in Saint-Laurent-sur-Mer by the 834th Air Engineer Battalion.

Within the vicinity of the front lines, the rudimentary Supply and Evacuation (S&E) airstrips were used to welcome C-47s, either to evacuate the wounded or to deliver supplies and ammunition. Rearming

and Refuelling Strips (R&R) enabled fighter planes and fighter-bombers to rapidly refuel and load ammunition. Advanced Landing Grounds (ALG), equipped with 1,200 and 1,700 metre-long and 40 metre-wide runways, in turn welcomed several tactical groups and medium bombers. Some of them were transformed into Tactical Air Depots (TAD).

Once cleared of mines and repaired, the airfields that were captured from the Germans, such as Carpiquet and Querqueville, were integrated within the Allied logistics. Built in just 14 days, the former could house a fleet of 220 C-47 Dakotas.

During critical battle phases, the Air Tactical Transport Command (USAAF) and the 46th Transport Command (RAF) brought material, ammunition, food and medication in from England, before transferring it to the front lines.

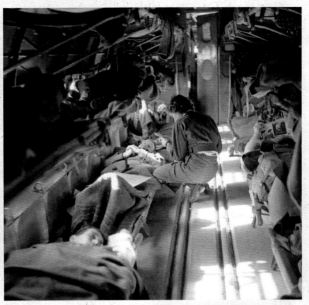

Wounded soldiers waiting to be evacuated to England aboard a C-47 Dakota on the 12th of June 1944. © NARA

Medical staff watching over the wounded during the crossing. © NARA

Armourers resupplying the Cal.50 machine gun racks aboard a P-47 Thunderbolt fighter plane. © NARA

AIRBORNE ENGINEERS

On the American side, the IX Engineer Command, part of the IX USAAF, reunited engineers and support units in charge of repairing existing airfields and building new runways. Created on the 30th of March 1944, it comprised 28 Air Engineer battalions, three of which were airborne, i.e. a total of 17,000 men. Brigadier General James Newman was in command of the unit. By late July, the American Air Engineers had built thirty airfields throughout Normandy.

**71 airfields
10,000 tonnes of SMT
2,000 tonnes of PSP
80,000 hectares of runway
90,000 servicemen**

The British had in turn, from the very early days, deployed five Royal Air Force mobile Airfield Construction Service (ACS) units throughout Normandy, to build airfields in the vicinity of the front lines. Yet the Germans' stubborn resistance forced the British Armies to modify their original plan. Thanks to their excellent sense of improvisation, the men from the ACSs built no less than eighteen airfields across the Caen plain.

To build airfields in country locations, the construction units had earthwork equipment at their disposal, such as bulldozers, scrapers and mechanical spades. Take-off strips were covered with square-mesh track, pierced steel planks and prefabricated hessian. The bases' access routes, aircraft parking zones, ammunition and fuel depots, workshops, pilots' and staff quarters were put up in around ten days.

Insignia of the IX Engineer Command.
© Author's collection

Printed insignia of the Airfield Construction Service.
© Author's collection

THE SERVICING COMMANDOS

The mission entrusted to the men from the Servicing Commandos consisted in defending the landing strips in the case of attack and in repairing and supplying planes. Each unit was composed of two technical officers and 148 non-commissioned officers and ordinary soldiers. Men were recruited on a voluntary basis from all branches of the Air Force.

The various groups landed on Gold Beach on the 7th of June. They worked in close collaboration with the Royal Engineers, building landing strips, roads and the generators required to illuminate the runways. They cleared the terrain of mines, refuelled planes, rearmed and repaired damaged craft, all under artillery fire from the *Luftwaffe*, particularly active by night. The Commanders left French soil early August to join other theatres in South-East Asia.

The 819th Engineer Aviation Battalion installing SMT track on the runway at the ALG A-6 airfield in Beuzeville. © NARA

Re-arming a Hawker Typhoon fighter-bomber in an airfield in July 1944. © Getty Images

Successions of Landing Ship
Tanks arriving at Omaha Beach
to unload their cargo of vehicles.
© NARA

CHAPTER 4

THE BATTLE OF LOGISTICS

Men from the 49th (West Riding) Infantry Division taking one of their wounded men to the rear during operation Epsom.

Early July, the Allies had landed 13 divisions, i.e. 1,000,000 men, 170,000 vehicles and 290,000 tonnes of material.

NORMANDY'S VERDUN

Recapturing Cherbourg had enabled the US First Army to redeploy its forces to the south. Montgomery asked Bradley to launch the offensive so that his troops could come within reach of the Lessay - Périer - Saint-Lô road. To the south if this line, the less cluttered landscape appeared more propitious to intervention by armoured divisions. The 1st US Army attacked along the leading road links: La Haye-du-Puits - Coutances, Carentan - Périers and Carentan - Saint-Lô. The Germans bitterly defended La Haye-du-Puis, Mont Castre and Sainteny. The GIs were to face a well-organised and fighting enemy, ready to impose a terrible war of attrition upon the Americans engaged in the heart of the Normandy bocage. In just 11 days, the VIII US Army Corps lost around 10,000 men. The town of Saint-Lô only fell into Allied hands on the 19th of July.

The battle was also raging to the north of Caen. The Germans had managed to stop the Anglo-Canadian troops in their tracks to the north and the west of the town. Montgomery launched several attacks to try to break through the enemy defences; however, they yielded disappointing results. Outflanking movements met with no greater success. The Germans had transformed the villages on the outskirts of Caen into entrenched camps. Tilly-sur-Seulles, Villers-Bocage, the Cairon-Authie-Bretteville-l'Orgueilleuse triangle, together with Hill 112, were all theatres of furious combat. On the 8th of July, the Anglo-Canadian troops forcefully penetrated inside Caen's north and west quarters, but it was only on the 19th that those located on the south bank of the Orne were reoccupied.

GIs waiting under the shelter of an embankment. The sticks were used to protect them from shrapnel and the airburst shells that exploded in the trees. © NARA

Two Canadian soldiers hollowing out their individual holes, strictly abiding by the instructions on the sign: 'Old soldiers never die, they dig. And fade away into a slit trench'.
© Library and Archives Canada

THE CLOSURE OF SWORD

Gooseberry G5 (Sword) was under enemy fire from German guns placed on the south bank of the Orne. A total of 32 ships and barges were hit. Under such conditions, only 1,600 tonnes of material and supplies could be handled daily. On the 15th of July, the decision was made to close the base and its personnel was sent to other Gooseberries. The port of Ouistreham resumed limited activity early September.

The Bayeux bypass.

ALLIED CAMPS AND DEPOTS

Engineer units were in charge of the depots and bases across Normandy. Thousands of tonnes of supplies, ammunition and weapons were landed and transported by truck to immense open-air depots. It was a tough task for these men to bring damaged road links and destroyed bridges and railway lines back into working order. Existing roads were widened and new roads were created from scratch across the fields.

Airfields, POW camps, maintenance and repair workshops, troop rest camps and field hospitals were installed in record time. The region was transformed into a massive hive of activity. The stagnating front forced the Allies to group their logistic infrastructures together near the beaches. They were close to each other due to the narrowness of the bridgeheads.

> **A field soldier needed 3 kg of supplies per day.**

The 2nd British Army's Army Ordnance Corps (RAOC), the Royal Army Service Corps (RASC) and their Canadian (RCOC and RCASC) and American (Quartermaster, Ordnance and Transportation Corps) counterparts were in charge of storage and transport. The vast majority of camps, depots and airfields were grouped around Bayeux. The British built a bypass to enable columns of vehicles to avoid the town. The RAOC's n°14 Advanced Ordnance Depot, built in Audrieu, covered a surface area of 25 hectares.

The 1st US Army gradually occupied the hinterland behind Omaha Beach and the Cotentin peninsula as the front advanced towards Cherbourg and Saint-Lô. Tens of thousands of jerrycans, tyres, engines, chests filled with food, ammunition and

Insignia of the Royal Electrical Mechanical Engineers.

A 1st US Army non-commissioned officer receiving a batch of brand new trousers for his supply corps men. © NARA

Norman civilians were used to handle goods in this US Army ammunition depot in La Cambe. © NARA

spare parts were piled up in depots located in Beach Maintenance Areas. In barely six weeks, four million square metres of storage space were created. These depots, some of which were only separated by a few hundred metres, had no camouflage. Automobile assembly lines were installed in La Cambe, Isigny and Querqueville. Every day, dozens of jeeps and GMC trucks were brought in, in parts and pieces, and assembled from start to finish. The daunting 150 metre-long and 40 metre-wide airship hangar in Ecausseville was used as a storage and maintenance centre for vehicles and tanks. Norman civilians were occasionally employed in workshops and depots.

Men from the Royal Electrical Mechanical Engineers changing the tracks of a Sherman tank. These units were capable of repairing vehicles damaged during combat directly on the roadside. © IWM

MATERIAL

Rhino ferries

These shallow draught barges measured 50 metres in length and 13 metres in width and were designed to unload LSTs, LCTs and cargoes moored offshore. Driven by two powerful outboard engines, they enabled ships to avoid long and laborious grounding manoeuvres. They were manned by the Seabees. From the 6th of June to the 21st of October 1944, they enabled some 94,495 vehicles and 422,195 tonnes of goods to be transhipped and unloaded onto Omaha Beach.

A Rhino ferry moving away from an LST once loaded. © NARA

The DUKW amphibious truck

The term DUKW designated the amphibious version of the 6x6 GMC CCKW 353 truck built as from 1942 by the General Motors Company under order from the US Army. This rather surprising 'boat on wheels' was driven by a propeller and equipped with pumps. Its driving wheels meant that it was at ease in a vast range of terrains. It could rapidly transport men and material from the ships offshore to the beaches. In Normandy, a total of 2,583 DUKWs were used by the Allied armies. Its payload capacity was 2.3 tonnes or 24 men. Over many long months, the amphibian truck companies assured continuous shuttles between the ships and the beaches, unloading thousands of tonnes of supplies, ammunition and weapons.

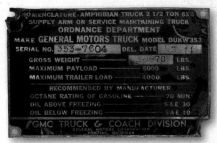

A fleet of DUKWs hurrying towards a cargo ship. © NARA

Number plate on a DUKW amphibious truck.
© Mémorial de Caen

Recovery tanks

The REME (Royal Electrical and Mechanical Engineers) deployed a total of 60 Sherman M4A2 BARVs (Beach Armoured Recovery Vehicles) to tow other vehicles that were either broken down or stuck in the sand. They were also occasionally used to drag grounded barges out of the sand. These entirely watertight vehicles, with a protuberant superstructure and devoid of turrets, could operate in a depth of up to 2.7 metres of water. The crew comprised a diver whose tasks included installing underwater towing chains. Although somewhat neglected in the honours, the BARVs played an important role on the Anglo-Canadian beaches. The British armoured divisions were equipped with Sherman M4 ARV (Armoured Recovery Vehicle) tanks from which the turrets had been removed. The Americans used M32 TRV (Tank Recovery Vehicle) tanks equipped with static turrets and 27-tonne hoisting cranes.

A BARV Sherman driving its way up a 13/18th Hussars column a few days before the Landings.

Bulldozers

Engineers units used civilian bulldozers for earthwork. The tilting blade, positioned by means of two hydraulic arms, enabled roads to be cleared, shell craters to be filled and airstrips to be created, all in record time. They were also used for towing vehicles and planes. The civilian vehicles produced by the Caterpillar Tractor Co (Model D7/D8) and by the International Harvester Co (Model TD18), were equally used by American and Anglo-Canadian units. In preparation for the D-Day Landings, some were armoured to protect both the driver and the engine. Sherman Dozer tanks were equipped with a blade mounted onto two arms that were attached to the track frame.

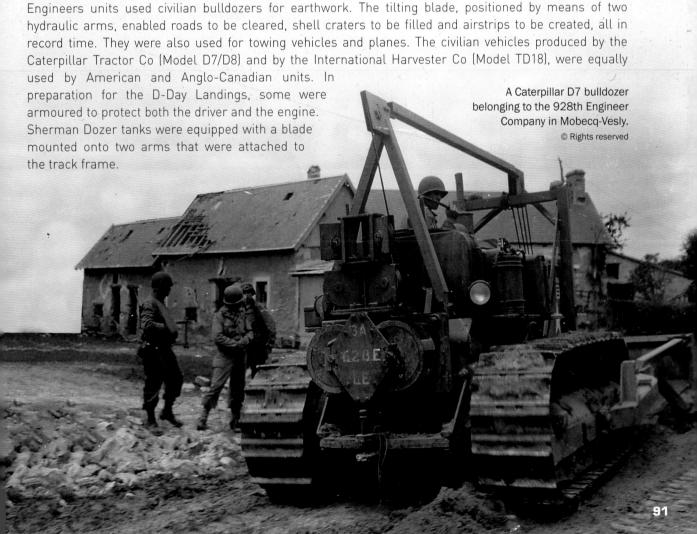

A Caterpillar D7 bulldozer belonging to the 928th Engineer Company in Mobecq-Vesly.

RATIONS

British rations

Each soldier was issued with one or two individual high-energy 24-Hour Rations, packaged in small, lightweight boxes. They included the following: dehydrated meat, porridge, biscuits, chocolate with raisins, sweets, tea, milk, sugar and stock. They were most often eaten warm, pending the arrival of Composite Ration Packs to feed 14 men. Packed in wooden chests, they were particularly appreciated thanks to their variety and the fact that they included ready-made canned meals. They came in seven different menus. Their contents could be distinguished via the use of the letters from A to G. The 5 in 1 ration was reserved for armoured crews. The Emergency Ration included 170 grammes of high vitamin content chocolate and was only to be eaten in the case of absolute necessity. To the rear, soldiers were issued with normal rations comprised of fresh, frozen or dehydrated produce, prepared by the Amercy Catering Corps' mobile kitchens.

The crew of a Cromwell tank from the 4th County of London Yeomanry preparing its meal on the 17th of June 1944.

Case of Compo rations and food supplies for the Anglo-Canadian armies.

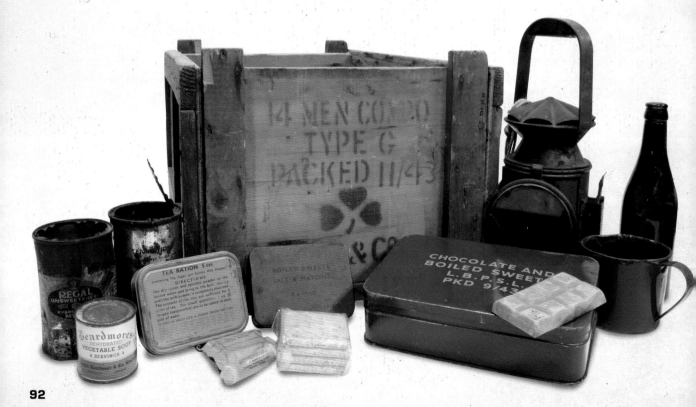

Afro-American soldiers loading 10 in 1 ration boxes aboard an LCI. © NARA

American rations

The American Field Ration was designed to be used occasionally by GIs. The type of ration differed depending on its purpose. They came in six distinct categories: C, K, D, B and A. Comprised of six cans, Field Ration C contained enough food for one day. This type of packaging enabled the menu to be varied.

Field Ration D, comprised of three high vitamin-content chocolate bars, was only to be used as a last resort and upon orders from an officer. It offered an energy value of 1,800 calories.

Field Ration K was developed upon request from the USAF and airborne forces. In 1942, its use was finally extended to include all US Army units. It comprised three boxes – one per meal: breakfast, dinner (lunch) and supper (dinner). The paraffined outside packaging was watertight and gastight. A complete ration weighed in at 1,300 to 1,400 grammes depending on its contents. In 1944, a total of 105 million rations were produced.

Field Rations B and A were designed to be consumed far from the combat zone. These more classical rations were also more fragile for they comprised freshly prepared ingredients. They were generally served in canteens. The 10 in 1 ration was designed to feed ten men. Available in five different menus, it was distributed in boxes or cases.

Each of the three boxes that comprised a K Ration weighed 400 grammes and provided an energy value of 3,900 calories per day. © Mémorial de Caen/Author's collection

MEDICAL SERVICES

Medical units were set up gradually. In the early days, the wounded were cared for by ambulance units that transferred them direct to advanced medical posts and, for the most serious cases, to sorting centres and advanced surgical centres in order for appropriate care to be administered. The wounded soldiers were then transferred to England by sea.

Each division had its own medical battalion (and airborne divisions their own company). Several specialised medical detachments (surgery, transfusion, laboratory, ambulances, etc.) were taken to theatres of operation in Normandy. Field hospitals followed behind the advancing front.

The very first 400-bed mobile field hospitals were set up in Normandy over the days immediately following the Landings. They were located in the vicinity of the front to allow the wounded to benefit from rapid care. Their surgical teams and operating theatres looked after the most serious cases. General hospitals, with a capacity of 1,500 beds, welcomed troops with more minor wounds and who were capable of reintegrating their units after a short hospitalisation. They also cared for men suffering from severe fatigue or nervous breakdowns.

An exhausted nurse from the 44th Evacuation Hospital leaving a tent after hours of work to save or to ease the wounded. © NARA

Omaha on the 12th of June - a column of jeeps taking the wounded to LST 134 for their evacuation to England. © NARA

RED GOLD

The Americans solved blood storage and conservation problems by cold-drying (by lyophilisation) plasma. Given the ever-increasing need for blood, Dr Charles R. Drew developed a plasma storage system (Blood Bank). The idea was also adopted by the British, who established mobile blood banks to facilitate the treatment of wounded soldiers. Plasma was transported from the United States to England by plane, in isothermal containers, then in refrigerated trucks towards refrigerated stores. A blood bank was set up in Bayeux. Although, to date, it had been practically impossible to bring blood to the battle field due to its rapid coagulation, the strict logistics set up by the Allies, including a cold supply chain, enabled this precious and perishable substance to be transported to transfusion stations and advanced sanitary posts with one aim in mind, 'that no wounded soldier may die from lack of blood'. They could now be transfused amidst the fray. Blood could also be parachuted in containers or sent inside hollow shells.

The interior of the LSTs was specially designed to welcome the wounded. © NARA

Once stabilised, patients were transferred to evacuation hospitals with 400 to 750 beds. In Normandy, the 1st US Army boasted a total medical staff of 30,760, six field hospitals and 22 evacuation hospitals. During the battle, some 56,000 patients were treated there.

Most of the British and Canadian military hospitals, referred to as field dressing stations, were coordinated by the 2nd British Army and concentrated around the Bayeux sector.

Sanitary trains also joined operations on a gradual basis, as and when the railway lines were repaired. The first train was operational on the 1st of August 1944 on the Cherbourg-Carentan line. Airborne sanitary transport also rapidly increased. It enabled some 20,000 GIs to be repatriated by the 31st of July. Sanitary planes also brought in medication and plasma. Patients were then evacuated by sea to the south coast of England aboard specially equipped LSIs and LSTs. Hospital ships, capable of transporting 300 to 400 wounded were also moored off the Normandy coast. The wounded were first taken to transit hospitals, set up near ports, before being transferred to general hospitals.

Advances and improvements in the medical care administered resulted in a significant decrease in mortality.

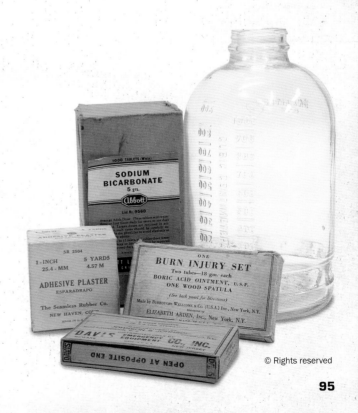

Partial view of the 5th General Hospital near Carentan. © NARA

THE US ARMY'S
5TH GENERAL HOSPITAL

Created in January 1942, the unit first landed in Southampton, to set foot on Norman soil on the 6th of July 1944. Its staff – 58 officers, 102 nurses and 500 men – was temporarily inactive for all its material had been landed in Cherbourg. Since Saint-Lô was still in enemy hands, they needed to find a new base to establish the hospital. In the meantime, most of the unit's staff members were sent to Cherbourg and to the 1st US Army's evacuation field hospitals. The others camped for around three weeks in Osmanville, in the company of the 7th Field Hospital. Then tents were finally pitched in Saint-Hilaire-Petitville to the east of Carentan and in the vicinity of the 50th General Hospital. Operational as from the 31st of July, the hospital treated a total of 4,238 patients the following month.

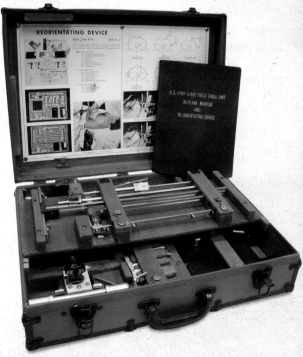

Case containing instruments for cardiothoracic surgery.
© Vassas collection/Author's collection

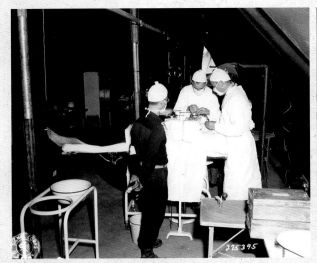

Three surgeons operating a patient. © NARA

Medical staff carefully stored and listed all medical products and equipment. © NARA

24th July – soldiers unloading the 5,000 elements required to set up the hospital. © NARA

11th June – prisoners helping to unload a Canadian
Ford F15 4 wheel-drive truck.

PRISONERS OF WAR

The Allied armies in Normandy were also responsible for the enemy soldiers taken prisoner during combat. On the early hours after the Landings, these prisoners were grouped together on the beaches before being evacuated by boat to Great Britain, where temporary camps had been set up. However, this preplanned evacuation did not prevent the Allies from using POWs for logistic tasks on the beaches. They evacuated the wounded, recorded and buried victims from both sides and even unloaded the boats they were due to board.

The Allies later created large POW camps (Central Continental Prisoner War Enclosures or CCPWEs), together with permanent labour camps to cope with the ever-increasing influx of new prisoners. The latter, located behind the front lines, could house up to 60,000 prisoners. Divided into work companies, the prisoners were used as labourers by the Anglo-Canadian troops. They cleared roads and participated in logistics (setting up camps, handling goods) and in mine clearing operations. Vital for the effective continuation of military operations, these tasks required extensive manpower, in particular due to the increasing distance between communication lines.

German soldiers and *Osttruppen* waiting on Utah Beach to be taken to England. © NARA

By the 21st of August 1944, the date that marked the closure of the Falaise Pocket, the Allied troops had captured a total of 177,000 *Wehrmacht* soldiers. By mid September, the number of prisoners had reached 355,000 prisoners. The camps established in Normandy housed a total of 75,000 enemy POWs of all nationalities.

German soldiers digging graves in a temporary military cemetery. © NARA

Afro-American soldiers stored jerrycans for use on the Red Ball Express. © NARA

AFRO-AMERICAN SOLDIERS

Supervised by white officers, the contingents of black soldiers were essentially reunited within units in charge of logistics (supplies, goods handling, kitchens, transport). Those who served in combat units were generally in artillery, engineer and anti-aircraft defence units. They collectively represented 5% of the US Army's total strength.

On the 6th of June, two of the 320th Anti-Aircraft Barrage Balloon Battalion's companies took part in the Landings by ensuring the protection of Omaha Beach. As from the 7th of June, certain Afro-American soldiers drove DUKWs, providing shuttle services between the ships and Omaha and Utah beaches, whereas others participated in the establishment of field hospitals and airfields.

In Cherbourg, black dockers from nine port battalions unloaded the Liberty Ships. These troops later joined Truck Companies, driving the trucks that transported ammunition and fuel to advanced divisions via the Red Ball Highway Express. Thanks to their work and their efforts to serve Allied logistics, Afro-American troops therefore contributed greatly towards victory.

In October 1944, 50,000 Afro-American soldiers were engaged in France. The 761st Tank Battalion (Black Panthers) was the first armoured unit to enlist these troops; it landed on Omaha Beach on the 10th of October 1944 to integrate General Patton's 3rd US Army. A total of 909,000 black soldiers served in the US Army.

Early August - men from the 374th Engineer General Service Regiment examining a German anti-tank mine. © NARA

Soldiers from the 320th Barrage Balloon Battalion installing VLA balloons above Omaha.
© NARA

RACIAL SEGREGATION IN THE US ARMY

The American armed forces practiced racial segregation, despite such practice having been strictly forbidden by the Selective Service Act, dated the 3rd of September 1940. This policy applied at all levels of military life. Afro-American soldiers were accommodated separately and went to different clubs and stores. Their quarters were generally insalubrious and most often located far from the white camps to avoid clashes. Food and military instruction were also of poor quality. The blood collected from Afro-American soldiers was stored separately and reserved for other black soldiers. Idleness, low education, alcoholism and casualness among the military authorities led to increasing cases of criminal behaviour (theft, rape, etc.) in the Cotentin peninsula. Black soldiers, particularly in force in the area, were designated by the local population and the military police as the leading culprits. Of a total of 86 sentences for rape, 80% were against black soldiers.

En Engineer installing a sign indicating the presence of booby traps inside a house. © NARA

BOOBY TRAPS

Making the absolute most of the adverse soldiers' natural curiosity and avidity, the German pioneers concealed explosive devices with internal detonation systems behind or under apparently inoffensive objects that were most likely to be used or moved by the Allies after the German retreat. An open door, an abandoned vehicle, a body, a wardrobe, a pack of beer or a pair of binoculars... could all be transformed into deadly traps. The charges they housed could either explode alone, or detonate other, more important charges such as shells or even aerial bombs.

Polish-designed MkI mine detector used by the British Army. © CDC Pays de Falaise collection/Author's collection

The Anglo-Canadian Engineers installed Bailey bridges to replace those destroyed in Caen.

Sappers repairing a road near Saint-Lô.

ENGINEER UNITS

Several Engineer battalions were engaged in Normandy. Their role included paving the way for the combat troops, by clearing and preparing the terrain. They were equally in charge of destroying obstacles and bunkers. Their tasks also included handling mines. These experts in explosives were faced with a tough task for their German counterparts had systematically mined and trapped inhabitations, transport and communication infrastructures and equipment, to thwart the Allied advance and to inflict losses. When troops found themselves in a defensive position, their mission was to hinder any enemy movement through the use of mines, barbed wire and fortified positions.

Behind the front lines, units specialising in military engineering were entrusted with a vast range of different tasks, including construction. They repaired bridges, roads, railway lines and even port facilities.

Insignia of the Royal Canadian Engineers.

BAILEY BRIDGES

For modern armies, destroying structural work is a huge obstacle during offensive phases. In May 1941, Donald Bailey, a British civil engineer from the Experimental Bridging Establishment, presented a prototype of a bridge that could be assembled and dismantled and that was of remarkably simple construction. The bridge elements, weighing in at just 272 kg, could be carried by just six men. The panels that comprised the main beams, weighing 202 kg, required four men. The Bailey bridge measured 21 metres in length and took just 36 minutes to install. The British Army installed 5,000 of these prefabricated bridges throughout Italy and Western Europe. No less than 17 Bailey bridges were installed across the River Orne and its canal during the summer of 1944. The US Army developed its own version under licence, referred to as the M2 bridge, of which it installed 1,000, despite lack of compatibility with the original version due to the larger deck.

Engineer units clearing the rubble that blocked the quayside - a perilous task due to the many mines left by the Germans. © NARA

American sappers ensuring the absence of concealed mines near the wreck of a *Panther Ausf. A* tank belonging to the *Panzer Lehr* and destroyed during operation Cobra. © NARA

BLACK GOLD FLOWING

Bringing in fuel supplies was one of the key priorities in the Overlord plan, as was the capture of continental ports and airfields. The Allies' needs in terms of fuel (petrol for vehicles, kerosene for aviation, diesel for ship engines) were colossal: 15,000 tonnes per day at D+41 (15th July).

Over the first week following the Landings, the absence of associated installations meant that jerrycans and petrol barrels were brought directly to the beaches aboard barges. A total of 2,000 tonnes of fuel were used daily and this empirical system only partly provided for the landed troops.

Meanwhile, the Navy set up the Minor System. From the 9th of June, a tanker anchor point linked by two sealines (flexible pipes laid on the sea bed) was installed off the shores of Sainte-Honorine-des-Pertes.

A double fuel terminal was installed on the interior quays of the Port-en-Bessin jetties. The Americans used the west sea wall and the British the east. Small 1,300-tonne tankers moored there to unload the precious liquid contained in their holds, as

A 1st Lieutenant from the Engineers opening a pipeline valve near Querqueville. © NARA

larger ships, anchored a few miles offshore connected to 6 inch / 15.2 cm (in diameter) and one mile-long pipelines that were kept at the water surface by means of buoys. The storage tanks were installed at the foot of the Vauban tower.

Royal Engineers installing infrastructures on the east pier in Port-en-Bessin. © NARA

The fuel stored in the tanks of this small tanker was pumped to be taken to the Étreham reservoirs.

The sealines and the fuel terminal were linked to a network of pipelines that fed the fuel reservoirs hastily set up on Mont Cauvin at a height of 68 metres. Fuel was sent from the hill, located to the east of Étréham, to Saint-Lô, by simple means of gravity and using no other mechanical system. The first deliveries began as from the 16th of June. The system, baptised Tombola, enabled 8,000 tonnes of fuel to be unloaded every day. By late August, a total of 175,000 tonnes of fuel had been transported.

This initial supply chain was scheduled to be stopped as from the 15th of July, to be replaced by installations, referred to as the Minor System, installed in Cherbourg.

'Civilians, please immediately return, either to your local council, or to the children entrusted with collecting them, all the 'jerrycan' containers you may find. Please do not give them direct to soldiers, you would only hinder progression of the convoys.'

SHAEF press release.

PRECIOUS TOOLS

This metallic container designed to transport and handle fuel was used by the German army from the very early days of the conflict. After careful study, the British and American forces decided to copy the German jerrycan, whilst improving it. The pouring hole was modified to adapt a flexible spout and an air intake was added so it could be emptied faster. The American canvas jerrycan had a capacity of 19 litres (5 gallons). Its name was the association of 'jerry' (the nickname given to German soldiers by the British) and the word 'can'. It was also used to transport drinking water. To avoid any confusion, the Germans painted white crosses and the British the letter 'W' on water cans.

In the autumn of 1944, the Allies faced a serious shortage of jerrycans. Many had been abandoned and recovered by civilians who then sold them back to the soldiers, full or empty. An estimated 15 million, of a total of 17 sent to Normandy since the 6th of June, were lost, hence posing a serious threat to the continuation of forwarding fuel supplies to the Allied divisions. Appeals were made to the general population by means of posters or through the press. School children were encouraged to recover the containers. Diplomas were even awarded to those who collected the largest numbers.

This American-made jerrycan was used to fuel flame throwers (Flame Thrower Fluid). Its destination (Utah) and manufacturing references are stencilled on the side. © Vassas collection/Author's collection

THE AMERICAN BREAKTHROUGH

Early July, the 1st US Army launched its offensive to the south, heading for La Haye-du-Puits and Saint-Lô. However, the GIs came across fierce resistance from the Germans who had come to master and fully exploit the complexities of the bocage landscape. Finally, on the 18th of July, after a week of bombardment, the 29th USID's vanguard reached the centre of the ruined town.

Operation Cobra was launched a week later. To the south of the D900 road between Saint-Lô and Périers, the first German lines were annihilated under Allied bombs. The American tanks thrust into the breach and headed southwards. After the failed German counter-attack in Mortain, the Americans entered Avranches on the 31st of July, to seize the miraculously intact Pontaubault bridge the following day.

US Army flask.

> **The tonnage unloaded on the American beaches reached its peak on the week from the 5th to the 11th of July 1944: 95,440 tonnes on Omaha and 65,004 tonnes on Utah, i.e. a total of 160,000 tonnes in seven days.**

General Patton's 3rd US Army then entered the scene. In three days, 120,000 men and 10,000 vehicles crossed the River Sélune before fanning out from the opposite bank. The VII US Army Corps reached Brittany as the XV US Army Corps launched a vast turning movement towards Paris, via Le Mans. France's liberation was in the making.

US Army shell container.

29th USID units entering Saint-Lô.

A 4th US Armoured Division column on its way through Avranches on the 31st of July 1944. © NARA

A convoy of Mack NO 6 wheel-drive trucks towing 155 mm Gun M1s (Long Tom) through Bagnoles-de-l'Orne. © NARA

A Sherbrooke Fusiliers Regiment Sherman tank entering Caen on the 10th of July 1944.

THE ENCIRCLEMENT

After successfully entering Caen on the 9th of July, the Anglo-Canadian troops liberated the south bank on the 19th of July. However, the German armoured divisions continued to defend the zone between Caen and Falaise.

On the 30th of July, the 2nd British Army launched operation Bluecoat to support the Americans on their left flank. Launched from Caumont-l'Éventé, the offensive targeted the town of Vire. Reinforced by two armoured divisions, the Germans bitterly defended the terrain, withdrawing in order towards Falaise and Alençon.

The Germans moved a large share of their armoured units to the west of the front, initially to counter the Cobra and Bluecoat offensives, then in support of the counter-attack in Mortain. The defences to the south of Caen had become dangerously weakened and the Falaise road seemed open. Reinforced by the 1st Polish Armoured Division, the 1st Canadian Army thrust forwards towards the 'stopper' in the wake of operations Totalize and Tractable. The Canadians reached Falaise on the 17th of August.

By August 1944, no less than 39 divisions were engaged on the Normandy front. Each of them consumed 700 to 750 tonnes of supplies per day, i.e. a total of 20,000 tonnes.

Infantrymen from the 43rd Wessex Division on Hill 112.

Montgomery and Bradley's troops were to join forces in Argentan, to the south of Falaise, then to trap the *7.Armee* and the *5. Panzerarmee*. However, a series of hitches hindered the closure of the pocket, which was finally achieved 10 km further east, between Trun and Chambois, around the 20th of August. Of the 150,000 soldiers from the Reich initially threatened by the encirclement, a third managed to escape the pocket before it was closed and as many to force the barrage held by the Polish at its exit, on the Mont Ormel heights. Despite the 40,000 prisoners and 5,000 to 6,000 victims, two thirds of the German troops managed to break out of the cauldron.

The Battle of Normandy came to an end a fortnight before General Eisenhower's forecast (D-Day+75 instead of D-Day+90). Two days later, the Americans from the 3rd US Army had already reached the Seine. The French General Leclerc's *2e Division Blindée* and the 4th US Infantry Division prepared to enter Paris.

The October 3rd issue of *Yank* magazine highlighting the American troops' arrival in Belgium. © Author's collection

Germans surrendering to the 4th Canadian Armoured Division on the 19th of August 1944 in Saint-Lambert-sur-Dives. © Library and Archives Canada

THE ALLIED ARMIES STILL HIGHLY DEPENDENT

To provide sufficient fuel supplies to the 200,000 vehicles engaged in the bridgehead and to ensure sufficient provisions based on average consumption for a fortnight, some 500,000 tonnes needed to be unloaded between the 6th of June and the 15th of July.

Overall, the Allied armies were sufficiently provided for during the Battle of Normandy. However, once the Falaise pocket had been closed, the Anglo-Canadian armies rapidly advanced towards northern France and Belgium, whilst the American units headed towards eastern France. Given the impossibility to exploit the Breton ports or Le Havre, the services in charge of supplies struggled to keep up with the sustained advance of the armoured divisions.

The needs were considerable. By late August, the American armies consumed 4 million litres of fuel per day and the Allied armies combined over 8 million litres. The communication lines, which had become considerably longer in just a few days, no longer enabled the leading Allied divisions to be correctly supplied in fuel.

Disillusioned, Patton had no choice but to stop his army's offensive in Meuse on the 31st of

COM-Z insignia. © Author's collection

Tractors towing articulated 7,600 litre tanks were the most frequently used vehicles for transporting fuel. © NARA

August, due to a fuel shortage for his tanks. The same day, his 3rd US Army only received 90 of the 1,155 tonnes required, for Eisenhower had decided to place priority on Montgomery's 21st Army Group, engaged in Belgium and the Netherlands. With the 3rd US Army stopped in its tracks, the Germans were able to re-establish their positions in Moselle.

The Allies needed to find solutions, and fast. The railway network was restored gradually in line with the Allied armies' advance; however, it took time to repair the destroyed lines, shunting points, stations and bridges.

To replace the French rail fleet, 1,323 locomotives and over 100,000 wagons were delivered. The aviation contributed to this effort. In September, 45,000 tonnes of fuel were transported by B-24 Liberator bomber and C-47 Dakota. In the meantime, roads remained the simplest and the fastest means of transport.

Men from the 3820th Quartermasters Gas Supply Company filling thousands of jerrycans in the La Cambe sector. © NARA

AVERAGE ALLIED VEHICLE CONSUMPTION PER 100 KILOMETRES

Willys Jeep: 12 litres.	GMC truck: 40 litres.	M26 Pacific Truck: 150 litres
Daimler Armoured Car: 17 litres.	M2 Half Truck: 95 litres.	M4A3 Sherman Tank: 235 litres.
Dodge WC 51 truck: 31 litres.	Bren Carrier: 70 litres.	Churchill Tank: 334 litres.

OPERATION BAMBI

The Minor System was progressively replaced by the Major System, offering a far greater volume. It required to be filled both by the large tankers moored at the Querqueville dock and via an underwater pipeline. Due to the scale of the destruction inflicted on port infrastructures, repair work needed to be completed before deploying the system. Allied planners had forecast that 90% of fuel would pass via Cherbourg at D+15. But it was only on the 25th of July, a month after the port's recapture, that the first tanker was able to moor on the quayside.

Installation of the HAMEL pipelines required quite considerable resources. These 112 kilometre-long pipes were rolled onto huge 27 metre-long and 12 metre-high 'Conum' reels. These 1,600-tonne floating giants, were towed by three tugboats at a speed of 7 to 10 knots. It took three cable ships equipped with reels in their centre to transport the HAIS. Installing this continuous pipeline from one to the other side of the Channel was to take no longer than 10 hours to avoid any hitches associated with the tide or the currents.

On the 12th of August, *HMS Latimer* and *HMS Sancroft* installed the first HAIS pipelines between Sandown Bay on the Isle of Wight and Urville-Nacqueville, near Querqueville, over two months after D-Day. The system was brought into effective service on the 18th of September: 52 bars of pressure provided a flow of 254 m³/day, i.e. half the forecast volume. Due to the concretions that had come to cover the lines installed under the sea six months previously, the first HAMEL pipeline was only brought into service on the 29th of September.

A network of pipes was also installed to take fuel to depots in La-Haye-du-Puits, Lessay, Saint-Lô and Vire to name but a few. A stock of 66 million litres was collected. The pipelines then followed the front lines. On the 25th of August, they reached Paris, then Rouen on the 30th and Antwerp on the 4th of September. A total of 8,900 kilometres of pipeline linked Normandy with the Paris basin. From the 6th of June to late August 1944, 5.2 million tonnes of fuel were transported across Normandy, 80% of them via the Minor System. By enabling tankers to unload directly within the land pipeline network,

A network of pipelines on the road to Port-en-Bessin. © NARA

Cherbourg and the other smaller Normandy ports were able to compensate for the inefficiency of Bambi, which had only enabled 379,000 tonnes to be brought in, i.e. 8% of the total.

It was replaced by the Dumbo system linking Dungeness with Ambleteuse in the Pas-de-Calais region. Eleven HAISs and six HAMELs transported 3,900 tonnes of fuel every day. The ports of Le Havre and Cherbourg continued to be supplied by tanker, as did Dieppe and Boulogne-sur-Mer. The Pluto system was dismantled a few months after the German capitulation.

Opinions on the success of Pluto diverged greatly. The Minor System had worked perfectly well, enabling the Allied armies to be sufficiently supplied, whereas the Major System, operating from Cherbourg, had been implemented far too late. The other pipelines, HAIS and HAMEL, deployed further north, thankfully yielded expected results. In January 1945, some 305 tonnes of fuel crossed

The tanker *Empire Traveller* unloading its cargo in Querque-ville. © NARA

the English Channel every day. By May, the figure had increased to 4,000 tonnes. A total of 781 million litres of fuel had travelled under the Channel from August 1944 to May 1945.

A Conum reel on the banks of the Thames.

Accidents were frequent on the RBE. This Federal 94x43 tractor has swerved off the road, without for as much stopping the traffic flow. © NARA

THE RED BALL EXPRESS

As from the 24th of August 1944, the US Army began to implement a road convoy system between Saint-Lô (linked to Cherbourg) and Chartres, to take supplies to the 3rd US Army's motorised columns, stopped in their tracks due to fuel shortage. Certain roads were specifically reserved for supply convoys

and a vast range of vehicles were used. Diamond M-20, GMC CCKW 353 and AFKWX-353 trucks, together with International M425 – H542-9, Federal 94x43, Autocar U7144T and Chevrolet G-4113 tractors set off from Saint-Lô to head for the depots that supplied advanced units. When the operation reached its peak, 132 transport companies, 6,000 trucks and 30,000 men were mobilised.

Men from the 1st ESB loading shell racks onto trucks in the Lison depot. © NARA

THE ADSEC

The Allied command established the COM-Z, a command centre in charge of communication routes. With a fleet of 5,000 vehicles and activated in February 1944, the 1st US Army's ASDEC (Advance Section Communications Zone) was in charge of controlling not only activities in the port of Cherbourg and on the beaches, but also those to the rear of the front lines. Its missions were to repair communication lines and to supply combat units. Fuel transport was of vital importance for the continuance of operations. However, the section's missions stretched well beyond fuel supply, for it was also in charge of the blood banks and the field hospitals behind the front.

'My soldiers can eat their waist belts, but my tanks need gas.'

General George S. Patton – August 1944.

This route, the direction of which was to evolve throughout the conflict, was baptised the Red Ball Express. Inspired from American railway line vocabulary, the term signified a priority delivery to be made without delay. Every day, 48-vehicle convoys took to the Express, by day and by night, along two one-way roads.

The road located furthest to the north was used by loaded trucks. Once unloaded, they made their return journey via the southern road. The drivers, most of whom were Afro-Americans (75%), were strictly forbidden to stop outside of the scheduled break periods. Large 'Today's Tonnage Target' signs informed them of the day's target in an aim to motivate the troops. Repair workshops, camps, fuel stations and control points were installed at regular intervals and civilian vehicles were banned from using these routes. Men, machines and roads were put to the test. The roads were in a poor state and

Red Ball Express insignia. The letters MTS stand for Colonel Loren Ayers' (from the COM-Z) Motor Transport System and the letters TC, Transportation Corps. © Author's collection

fatal accidents were far from rare. In order to limit the risk of collision, drivers were given extremely strict instructions. They were to leave a distance of 70 yards (64 metres) between trucks and to drive at a speed limit of 40 km/h.

Over its first weeks, the Red Ball Express (RBE) was as yet in its infancy and the quantities of fuel

A column of heavily laden GMC CCKW-353 trucks belonging to the ASCZ as it sets off. A network of pipelines can be seen on the verge. © NARA

In the autumn of 1944, heavy rain and passing trucks transformed the roads into quagmires. Yet, the GMCs kept going. © NARA

Manual for GMC drivers. © Author's collection

THE GMC CCKW 352/353

Within the framework of the US Army's equipment and standardisation plan, the Quartermaster Corps chose the 2.5-tonne 6-wheel drive truck produced by the Yellow Truck & Coach Company, which later integrated General Motors. Production was launched late 1941. The GMC CCKW 353, an adaptation of an existing commercial model, was a well-equipped, robust and reliable vehicle at ease in all terrains thanks to its three driven beam axles. The vehicle was equally used by the US Army and by other Allied forces. The troops nicknamed the GMC *Jimmy*. Whilst its cargo bed with slatted sides could transport 2.5 tonnes of freight or 10 fully-equipped men, the vehicle could push its capacity to 5 tonnes. It came in different versions - tank trucks, tipper trucks - or equipped with shelter radio or even a workshop. The short wheelbase version of the CCKW 352 was designed to transport artillery pieces. The *Jimmies* were the very backbone of the American logistic success.

GMC steering wheel.

effectively delivered were insufficient to keep up with the pace of the US divisions. Providing sufficient food and ammunition supplies was also proving complicated. However, the situation gradually improved and the Red Ball Express finally operated at full capacity. The US Army logisticians applied the 'just in time' principle, first adopted by Ford in the 1930s, relying, in particular on the resumption of rail transport. On the 18th of September, a record 9,024 tonnes of goods of all sorts were transported. By late September, Patton's units received 1,450 tonnes of fuel per day. In just 82 days, drivers transported a total of 412,197 tonnes between Cherbourg and the towns of Dreux and Chartres. The US Army's umbilical cord in France finally closed on the 16th of November 1944.

Concurrently, other, less imposing logistics circuits were also implemented. Opened from the 6th of October 1944 to the 10th of January 1945, the White Ball Express Highway linked the ports of Le Havre and Rouen with the advanced ASDEC depots around Reims. The Red Lion Express, set up in September between Bayeux and Brussels, enabled 500 tonnes of goods to be transported every day in support of operation Market Garden. In October, the Green Diamond Route was opened by the Normandy Base Section to transport goods to Brittany (Granville and Dol). During the Battle of the Ardennes, the Little Red Ball enabled 100 tonnes of supplies to be brought from the Cotentin peninsula to the Parisian railway stations in less than 24 hours. In September, the Toot Sweet Express, a 20-wagon priority train transported 385 tonnes of freight and mail per day between Cherbourg and the Advance Section bases, via Paris.

Bottles of blood and boxes of penicillin being unloaded in Holland on the 5th of October 1944.

Corporal C.H. Johnson from the 783rd MP Battalion readily posing beside a sign indicating the daily tonnage transported along the Red Ball Highway.

Military Police helmet, armband and whistle.

THE CIGARETTE CAMPS

The increasing distance from the front obliged the American high command to progressively abandon Cherbourg in favour of other ports closer to the front lines. In the autumn of 1944, vast military camps were established within the immediate vicinity of the port of Le Havre, which became the Americans' leading European logistics base. A total of eight of these camps were set up on the Le Havre heights, in the Pays de Caux and near Rouen. They initially served as transit camps for the soldiers engaged in combat units who had just landed in France. For safety reasons, each camp was named after a brand of cigarettes. The zone was placed under General Finley's orders, with its headquarters in Bois-Guillaume near Rouen.

Over the early months, living conditions in these camps remained rudimentary. In the midst of winter, soldiers were accommodated in canvas tents, pitched between mud filled alleys and devoid of any sanitary facilities. Early 1945, the tents were replaced by wooden (Tropical Wood model) or metallic (Nissen model) barracks, the alleys were asphalted and their square plan as straight as a die. The wider alleys were named after American towns

GIs looking at a sign indicating the distance between Le Havre and the major cities in America and in Texas.
© NARA

or the principal Allied leaders. Camps comprised not only all the necessary services (sanitary facilities, kitchens, hospitals, repair workshops), but also theatres, cinemas, bars, sports grounds, PX stores supplied with American products, Catholic chapels and Protestant churches. German POWs were utilised in these camps, in the kitchens in particular. The capacity of these camps gradually increased. For example, Camp Lucky Strike housed 11,600 tents and barracks, 4 hospitals, several cinemas and a landing strip, all covering a total surface area of 600 hectares.

After Germany's capitulation, the American soldiers were gathered together in cigarette camps pending their demobilisation or transfer to the Pacific.

From October 1944 to August 1946, 3.67 million American soldiers travelled via the port of Le Havre. Similar camps were installed near the ports of Marseille (Delta Base Section) and Antwerp (Camp Tophat).

Lucky Strike
(Saint-Valéry-en-Caux):
58,000 men

Philip Morris
(Gonfreville-l'Orcher):
35,000 men

Twenty Grand
(Saint-Pierre-de-Varengeville):
20,000 men

Old Gold
(Fauville-en-Caux):
20,000 men

Herbert Tareyton:
16,400 men

Pall Mall (Étretat): 7,700 men

Wings (Bléville): 2,250 men

Home Run (Sanvic):
2,000 men

A Nissen hut camp.

US Navy LSTs unloading directly onto the beach in Le Havre. The American logistics were on a just-in-time basis. tendu.

OVERALL RESULT

With the increase in traffic via Cherbourg and the capture of new port infrastructures (Granville, Morlaix, Le Havre, Dieppe, Ostende), the small Norman ports eventually ceased to be used mid September and were restored to the French authorities on the 9th of November 1944. The Gooseberries ceased all activity at the same time.

Via the beaches and the small American ports, some 2 million tonnes of supplies, 1.6 million men and 287,500 vehicles were unloaded in 24 weeks. The port of Cherbourg in turn handled one million tonnes as from its first day of operation on the 16th of July. The British port infrastructures dealt with 1.45 million tonnes, 739,000 men and 120,300 vehicles in 18 weeks.

The American Gooseberries yielded quite impressive results. The capacity of the port of Cherbourg rapidly increased and the small Norman ports provided a considerable contribution given their own, limited capacities. Although the results achieved by the artificial harbour in Arromanches may, on the surface, seem disappointing, they need to be put into perspective.

Indeed, the construction of prefabricated ports to supply the future bridgeheads on the European continent played a vital role in the Allied decision-making process. The Mulberry project was to considerably sway the Allied heads of state and their military chiefs as to the feasibility of the Normandy Landings. From their design to their installation, the Mulberries were the materialisation of genuine industrial and technological prowess. Although the

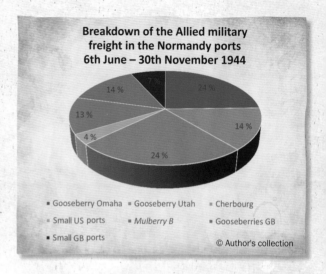

Breakdown of the Allied military freight in the Normandy ports 6th June – 30th November 1944

7 % · 24 % · 14 % · 14 % · 13 % · 4 % · 24 %

- Gooseberry Omaha
- Gooseberry Utah
- Cherbourg
- Small US ports
- *Mulberry B*
- Gooseberries GB
- Small GB ports

© Author's collection

37% of supplies, 23 % of men and 14% of vehicles belonging to the 2nd British Army entered France via Mulberry B on the Arromanches beach.

Saint-Laurent-sur-Mer harbour was unable to prove its worth, Port Winston put up a creditable performance. It compensated for the absence of a deep-water port and solved the problem of the shortage of barges and coasters among the Allied navies. The British harbour provided a safe haven for unloading large transport ships without requiring offloading. The evacuation of military staff, the wounded in particular, was made possible and in excellent conditions. It should also be highlighted that, whereas the US Army had continued to increase its strength up to the end of the year 1944, the Anglo-Canadian armies had landed virtually all their combat divisions by the end of August. The logistic needs of these armies evolved differently as from mid July. Neither the US Army nor its British and Canadian counterparts ever lacked in weapons, ammunition, food supplies or medication. Their logistics were adapted to suit their needs and this is most likely the essential point to bear in mind.

Mulberry B was used up to the 12th of October by the British who then conceded its use to the Americans for a few weeks.

© Author's collection

A further 19,000 tonnes of supplies were unloaded up to its permanent closure on the 19th of November.

Yet the harbour's story did not end there. Dismantling of the platforms and floating causeways began the following month. Four Phoenix caissons were sent to Le Havre to be used to rebuild the quays. Several other caissons were towed to Walcheren Island to fill the gaps in the polder sea wall caused by bombardments. The last caissons were stored

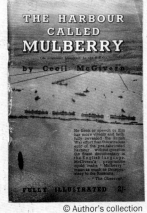

THE HARBOUR CALLED **MULBERRY**
by Cecil McGivern

FULLY ILLUSTRATED 2/-

© Author's collection

in Portland before being transferred to Schouwen-Duiveland Island in 1953, also to repair the sea wall. Over the years that followed, other elements conceded to France, the Whale piers in particular, were used to repair or replace destroyed structural works throughout France and in other countries. The same applied to the Bailey bridges.

This book will have offered you an insight into the extraordinary story, not only of the Allied harbours that comprised the Pluto system, of the Red Ball Express, the Allied camps and bases established in Normandy, but also of the men and women who strove to offer precious assistance and support to their compatriots fighting on the front lines. None of this would have been possible without them.

© NARA

No wonder they call it *The "Duck"*

Amphibious action is playing an ever increasing part in World War II. And the 2½-ton Amphibian truck, now in volume production at GMC Truck & Coach Division factories, is giving American Armies an ever increasing advantage over the Axis. In the water, it has all the qualities of a large landing boat, *plus* the ability to keep going when it reaches shoals and shore line. On land, it provides performance comparable to a GMC "six by six" army truck, *plus* the ability to swim lakes and streams. Carrying cargoes from ocean freighter to inland supply depot . . . establishing beach heads and bridge heads . . . unloading ships where no harbor facilities are available . . . aiding in reconnaissance work where no roads or bridges exist . . . carrying or pulling cannon and howitzers . . . transporting scores of troops or tons of equipment . . . are all in a day's work for this sturdy, seagoing truck. No wonder the GMC workers helping to build it, and the soldiers using it, both call it the "Duck." It's one of America's most vital and versatile military vehicles!

INVEST IN VICTORY... BUY WAR BONDS AND STAMPS

GMC TRUCK & COACH DIVISION · GENERAL MOTORS

Home of GMC Trucks and GMC Coaches . . . Manufacturer of a Wide Variety of Military Vehicles for our Armed Forces

★ ★ ★

BIBLIOGRAPHY

BRITISH AIR MINISTRY (1944): *Evidence in camera, Special edition, The illustrated story of Mulberry B, 8(9).*

AUBIN, Nicolas (2014). *Les Routes de la liberté.* Paris, Histoire & Collections.

BENAMOU, Jean-Pierre (2014). *10 millions de tonnes pour une victoire.* Bayeux, OREP.

BAUDUIN, Philippe (2004). *Normandie 1944, Quand l'or noir coulait à flots.* Saint-Martin-des-Entrées, Heimdal.

BAUDUIN, Philippe (2007). *L'Or rouge, Les Alliés et la transfusion sanguine, Normandie 44.* Saint-Martin-des-Entrées, Heimdal.

CROCHET, Bernard (2008). *L'Effort de guerre américain.* Strasbourg, Éditions R. Hirlé.

FERRAND, Alain (2004). *Arromanches, histoire d'un port.* Bayeux, OREP.

HARTCUP, Guy (2011). *Code name Mulberry, The planning building and operation of the Normandy harbours.* Barnsley, Pen & Sword Military.

QUELLIEN, Jean (2012). *Les Américains en Normandie.* Bayeux, OREP.

QUELLIEN, Jean (2015). *Le Jour J et la bataille de Normandie.* Bayeux, OREP.

LECORNU, Gérard (2006). *Il faut sauver le port d'Arromanches.* Strasbourg, Éditions R. Hirlé.

LEE, Ulysse (1966). *The Employment of negro troops.* Washington, D.C., Office of the Chief of Military History, US Army.

PETERS, Brett (2012). *Mulberry-American, The artificial harbor at Omaha.* BiblioScholar.

ROBINARD, François (2012). *50 aérodromes pour une victoire. Juin-septembre 1944.* Saint-Martin-des-Entrées, Heimdal.

RUPPENTHAL, Roland G. (1953/1959). *Logistical support of the armies.* Washington, D.C., Office of Chief Military History, US Army.

STANFORD, Alfred B. (1951). *Force Mulberry, The planning and installation of the artificial harbor of US Normandy beaches in World War II.* Cambridge, Whitehead Press.

ZALOGA, Steven J. (2003). *D-Day 1944 : Omaha Beach.* Oxford, Osprey Publishing.

ZIEGELMANN, Fritz (1948). *Die Geschichte der 352. Infanterie-Division, MS B-741.*

ICONOGRAPHICAL RESOURCES

Library and Archives Canada
Imperial War Museum
Library of Congress
US National Archives
Mémorial de Caen
Private archives and collections

INTERNET RESOURCES

www.6juin.omaha.free.fr
www.history.army.mil
www.archives.gov

ACKNOWLEDGEMENTS

The author would like to thank the collectors and the staff members of the Arromanches Museum for their contribution towards the production of the present work, in particular Guillaume Dormy and Frédéric Sommier.

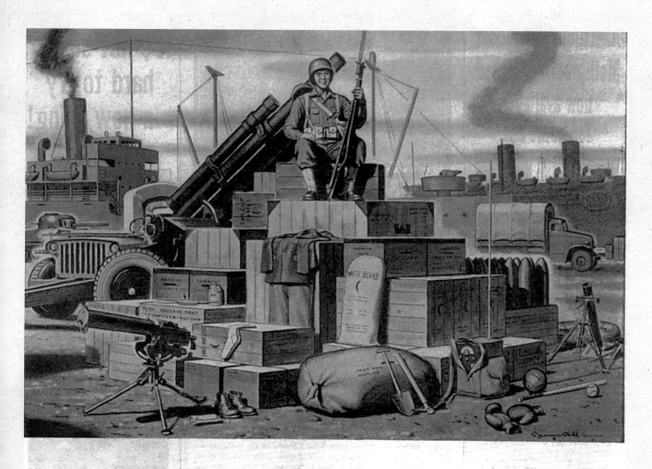

G.I. Joe and his 12 tons of baggage

Advertisement in the American magazine "Life" dating from July 1944 indicating that behind every GI, 12 tons of baggage was necessary

Advert in the July 1944 issue of Life Magazine indicating that behind each GI, there were 12 tonnes of luggage.

OREP
EDITIONS

Zone Tertiaire de NONANT - 14400 BAYEUX
Tel.: (33) 02 31 51 81 31 - **Fax:** 02 31 51 81 32
E-mail: info@orepeditions.com - **Website:** www.orepeditions.com
Editor: Grégory Pique - **Editorial coordination:** Joëlle Meudic - **English translation:** Heather Inglis
Graphic design - Layout: Antoine Salmon - **OREP éditions**